COLLEG

MANAGING FINANCIAL RESOURCES

**Managing Universities and Colleges:
Guides to Good Practice**

Series editors:

David Warner, Principal and Chief Executive, Swansea Institute of Higher Education

David Palfreyman, Bursar and Fellow, New College, Oxford

This series has been commissioned in order to provide systematic analysis of the major areas of the management of colleges and universities, emphasizing good practice.

Current titles:
Frank Albrighton and Julia Thomas (eds): *Managing External Relations*
Allan Bolton: *Managing the Academic Unit*
Ann Edworthy: *Managing Stress*
Judith Elkin and Derek Law (eds): *Managing Information*
John M. Gledhill: *Managing Students*
Christine Humfrey: *Managing International Students*
Colleen Liston: *Managing Quality and Standards*
Harold Thomas: *Managing Financial Resources*
David Watson: *Managing Strategy*

MANAGING FINANCIAL RESOURCES

Harold Thomas

Open University Press
Buckingham · Philadelphia

Open University Press
Celtic Court
22 Ballmoor
Buckingham
MK18 1XW

email: enquiries@openup.co.uk
world wide web: www.openup.co.uk

and
325 Chestnut Street
Philadelphia, PA 19106, USA

First Published 2001

A catalogue record of this book is available from the British Library

ISBN   0 335 20444 9 (pb)   0 335 20445 7 (hb)

Library of Congress Cataloging-in-Publication Data
Thomas, Harold (Harold George), 1945–
  Managing financial resources / Harold Thomas.
    p. cm. – (Managing universities and colleges)
  Includes bibliographical references and index.
  ISBN 0-335-20445-7 – ISBN 0-335-20444-9 (pbk.)
    1. Education, Higher–Great Britain–Finance. 2. Universities and colleges–Great Britain–Finance. I. Title. II. Series.

LB2342.2.G7 T46 2001
378.1'06'0941–dc21

                              2001021068

Typeset in 9/11pt Stone Serif by Graphicraft Limited, Hong Kong
Printed in Great Britain by The Cromwell Press, Trowbridge

CONTENTS ∎

3 **Institutional issues** 35

4 **The allocation process 1: understanding
the income** 57

5   **The allocation process 2: strategic and
    institutional considerations**   72

6   **The allocation process 3: distribution of
    resources**   88

7   Monitoring   108

Brian Lewis

8 Departmental perspective 140

Jointly authored with Peter Hodson

9 Consolidation 152

SERIES EDITORS'
INTRODUCTION

Post-secondary educational institutions can be viewed from a variety of different perspectives. For most of the students and staff who work in them they are centres of learning and teaching in which the participants are there by choice and consequently, by and large, work very hard. Research has always been important in some higher education institutions, but in recent years this emphasis has grown, and what for many was a great pleasure and, indeed, a treat, is becoming more of a threat and an insatiable performance indicator, which just has to be met. Maintaining the correct balance between quality research and learning/teaching, while the unit of resource continues to decline inexorably, is one of the key issues facing us all. Educational institutions as work places must be positive and not negative environments.

From another aspect, post-secondary educational institutions are clearly communities, functioning to all intents and purposes like small towns and internally requiring and providing a similar range of services, while also having very specialist needs. From yet another, they are seen as external suppliers of services to industry, commerce and the professions. These 'customers' receive, *inter alia*: a continuing flow of well qualified, fresh graduates with transferable skills; part-time and short course study opportunities through which to develop existing employees; consultancy services to solve problems and help expand business; and research and development support to create new breakthroughs.

However, educational institutions are also significant businesses in their own right. One recent study of the economic impact of higher education in Wales shows that it is of similar importance in employment terms to the steel or banking/finance sectors. Put another way, Welsh higher education institutions (HEIs) spend half a billion pounds annually and create more than 23,000 full-time equivalent jobs. And it must be remembered that there are only 13 HEIs in Wales, compared with 171 in the whole of the UK, and that these Welsh institutions are, on average, relatively small. In addition, it has recently been realized that higher education in the UK is a major export industry with the added benefit of long-term financial and political returns. If the UK further education sector is also added to this equation, the economic impact of post-secondary education is of truly startling proportions.

Whatever perspective you take, it is obvious that educational institutions require managing and, consequently, this series has been produced to facilitate that end. The editors have striven to identify authors who are distinguished practitioners in their own right and, indeed, can also write. The authors have been given the challenge of producing essentially practical handbooks that combine appropriate theory and contextual material with many examples of good practice and guidance.

The topics chosen are of key importance to educational management and stand at the forefront of current debate. Some of these topics have never been covered in depth before and all of them are equally applicable to further as well as higher education. The editors are firmly of the belief that the UK distinction between these sectors will continue to blur and will be replaced, as in many other countries, by a continuum where the management issues are entirely common.

For well over a decade, both of the editors have been involved with a management development programme for senior staff from HEIs throughout the world. Every year the participants quickly learn that we share the same problems and that similar solutions are normally applicable. Political and cultural differences may on occasion be important, but are often no more than an overlying veneer. Hence, this series will be of considerable relevance and value to post-secondary educational managers in many countries.

Perhaps after at least the maintenance and preferably the steady enhancement of academic quality, without which any university or college ceases to justify its existence and becomes a travesty, the next crucial aspect of managing the HEI is the maintenance of financial stability and indeed the promotion of financial flexibility that comes with a broad diversification of income sources, without which any university or college faces being unable to achieve the prime objective already mentioned. Hence we are pleased that Harold Thomas, once Deputy Registrar and then Financial Planning Manager at the University of Bristol and subsequently

Academic Registrar at Essex, has been willing to contribute this volume.

Those managing HEIs at whatever level – centre, faculty, school, department, academic unit – need to be familiar with the nitty-gritty of routine financial practice and with the basic principles of accurate costing, as well as with the way financial planning and projections need to mesh neatly and credibly with the marketing, personnel and infrastructure projections when pulling together the overall HEI strategic plan (see Watson, *Managing Strategy*) or the departmental business plan as a component of the HEI master-plan (see Bolton, *Managing the Academic Unit*). Thoroughly digesting this book is a good start to discharging one of the HE manager's prime duties of competence, while the extensive referencing and further readings cited will enable the colleague already past the early stages of expertise to follow up specialist needs and interests.

Before leaving the reader to enjoy, learn and implement, however, it is worth noting one very wise piece of prudent financial guidance supplied in 1379 to New College, Oxford, by its Founder (William of Wykeham, Bishop of Winchester and Lord Chancellor), and one still utterly pertinent to this day: one of Wykeham's Rubrics within the Statutes was that, when contemplating new academic activities, it will always be necessary as a matter of financial rigour to halve the income initially projected as flowing from the attractive new venture, while at the same time doubling the expected costs of resourcing this exciting initiative. If the sums still add up, then go ahead.

David Warner
David Palfreyman

NOTES ON AUTHOR AND CONTRIBUTORS

Harold Thomas is an education consultant working in the UK and internationally on issues of policy advice and capacity building. He was previously a senior university administrator with responsibilities in the areas of academic administration, strategic planning and financial management. His PhD is in the field of resource allocation.

Peter Hodson joined the University of Glamorgan (previously the Polytechnic of Wales) in 1982 after working for ten years with ICL. He was appointed Head of the School of Computing in 1989 and also Dean of Quality Assurance in 1997.

Brian Lewis is a chartered public finance accountant with over 20 years' experience in the financial aspects of education management. Currently Director of Finance at Swansea Institute of Higher Education, he holds a doctorate from Cardiff University. His research interests centre on delegated financial management in higher education.

LIST OF FIGURES
AND TABLES

Figures

Tables ▮

SELECTED ABBREVIATIONS ■

ABRC	Advisory Board for the Research Councils
APA	Association of Polytechnic Administrators
API	age participation index
AUA	Association of University Administrators
CIMA	Chartered Institute of Management Accountants
CIPFA	Chartered Institute of Public Finance and Accounting
CUA	Conference of University Administrators
CUC	Committee of University Chairmen
CVCP	Committee of Vice-Chancellors and Principals
DES	Department of Education and Science (renamed Department for Education, and now Department for Education and Employment)
DfEE	Department for Education and Employment
EU	European Union
HEFCE	Higher Education Funding Council for England
HEFCW	Higher Education Funding Council for Wales
HEIFES	Higher Education in Further Education: Students Survey
HEQC	Higher Education Quality Council
HESES	Higher Education Students Early Statistics Survey
ICAEW	Institute of Chartered Accountants in England and Wales
LEA	local education authority
LMS	local management of schools
MASNs	maximum aggregate student numbers
NAB	National Advisory Body for Local Authority Higher Education
NAO	National Audit Office

PAC	Public Accounts Committee
PCFC	Polytechnics and Colleges Funding Council
QAA	Quality Assurance Agency
RAE	research assessment exercise
SSR	staff/student ratio
UFC	Universities Funding Council (replaced by the Higher Education Funding Councils)
UGC	University Grants Committee (replaced by the Universities Funding Council)
VAT	value added tax

1

INTRODUCTION

Aims and objectives

The overall objective of the book is to provide a practical guide that will be of interest and help to a wide range of potential readers. The title, *Managing Financial Resources*, is deliberately chosen to cover what may be considered as two different but interrelated topics: financial management and resource allocation. The former refers to mechanisms for ensuring efficient and effective use of available funds, whilst the latter is concerned with the way in which resources are allocated to, or within, the component parts of an institution. Clearly the two concepts are closely related, for if the process of resource allocation is not based on sound principles, particularly of accountability, the chances of being able to establish effective systems of financial management are lessened.

Within this overall objective there will be a number of aims:

1 to outline how approaches to financial management have changed in line with changing government policies and other external pressures;
2 to identify types of funding and their sources;
3 to identify different ways in which resources are managed, including a comparison between central systems and devolved systems;
4 to review the mechanisms by which institutions allocate resources to their constituent parts. A distinction will be drawn between historic and formulaic systems;
5 to identify the staff involved in the financial management process;
6 to consider issues relating to the control of expenditure;
7 to review the relationship between institutional culture and financial management, both from the perspective of how the prevailing

culture can influence resource allocation methodologies and how those methodologies can be used to change the existing culture;

8 to consider the impact of different financial management systems on the power structure of institutions and on behaviour patterns of individuals and institutions;

9 to review, in the context of different financial management systems, issues of staff training and development, use of technology and institutional structures;

10 to consider the impact of different systems of financial management on administrative and managerial staff, in particular those in finance offices;

11 to consider the impact of resource allocation systems on the relationship between academic and administrative staff; and

12 to review the process of financial management in the context of institutional planning.

There is one further objective that should be mentioned. Many of the practices and procedures developed in response to environmental trends are common between different educational sectors and have become international in scope. As in other walks of life, however, the ways in which finances are managed are not immune from the fads and fashions of their times. It is intended, therefore, to look beneath and beyond what may be the current flavour of the month and to stimulate further thinking and perhaps provide a guide to additional reading.

Readership and approach ■

Institutional staff

Perhaps this is an appropriate point for a word of warning, or perhaps relief. It is not intended to delve into the detail of accounting practices. The management of financial resources involves not only financial specialists, but also a wide range of both academic and non-academic staff. Anyone working in the sector will be all too well aware of how financial constraints and changes in government policy have impacted on the management of institutions and on the daily lives of staff. Long gone are the days when issues of financial management were the sole preserve of colleagues in the finance section. Staff assuming any level of managerial responsibility who might still think in such terms will quickly realize that the well-being of their particular area is going to depend upon the gaining of a rapid familiarity with their institution's financial policies and practices, especially in the areas of resource allocation and incentive schemes. This necessity to become involved in issues of financial management has been particularly evident in the areas of academic activity. Regrettable as some may think it is, it has become a fact of life that deans and heads of department have to be as adept at financial management as at academic leadership (see Bolton 2000).

Whilst the issues discussed in the following pages are central to the role of staff in finance sections, the subject matter and approach adopted are aimed at a much wider audience. That is not to say, however, that the role of the financial specialist has become less important. Indeed, in many respects it has become more onerous. As financial responsibility has become more diffuse, the role of financial specialists has had to become more facilitative. Whilst maintaining control over appropriate practices and procedures and ensuring effective reporting and monitoring procedures, there has grown a more interpersonal and advisory function to support academics in departments and faculties with a financial responsibility. This has had implications for the organization, structure and culture of finance offices. Such issues are matters for later consideration.

Other stakeholders

So far the focus has been on the wide range of staff within institutions who are now involved in the process of financial management. Although the book, and indeed the series, is about key issues in institutional management, that does not imply that only institutional managers are the target audience. It is increasingly recognized that a wide range of stakeholders has an interest in higher education. This is not the place to consider at length the changing balance between institutional autonomy and public accountability, but there can be little doubt that there has been a trend towards greater accountability which has found expression in procedures of financial management and quality assurance (see Liston 1999). These trends have accompanied, and are a by-product of, the move from an elite to a mass system of higher education. If higher education is to be geared towards contributing to economic and social objectives, it is understandable that the products of the system will be subject to external influence. That influence may be exercised by employers, politicians, members of funding bodies, local business and commercial interests, parents of current or potential students, careers advisers, school and further education staff as well as those more directly involved, whether they be staff or students. Some of those stakeholders will find themselves as members of councils or boards of governors with a responsibility for the governance of their institution. The more those stakeholders understand the sorts of issue which confront institutional managers on a daily basis the more informed and valuable will be their contribution to the various debates in which they are involved.

Whilst it is clearly intended that institutional managers will themselves find here valuable source material, it is also intended that the presentation and discussion of the various issues will be undertaken in such a way as to be interesting to readers who may not themselves be employed by an educational institution but who have an interest in how such institutions are run. They may already have a direct responsibility for the well-being of an institution as a lay governor or member of council, or they may be involved as an employer or member of the local community. Perhaps even students and their parents will be able to dip into the pages and learn a little more about some of the complex and sometimes bewildering aspects surrounding the management of financial resources which is but a part of the world of higher education management.

International dimension

Before leaving the issues of readership and approach and moving to discuss some of the contextual issues that have influenced institutional financial management reference needs to be made to the international dimension of the book. The book is primarily written from the perspective of the UK system. There are, however, many international trends in higher education. Transfer of practices between nations and between systems can be fraught with difficulty because of different cultural assumptions, nevertheless there is a certain commonality in governmental approaches and institutional responses. These issues will be considered in more detail below, but for the present it is enough to express the hope that there will be issues here of interest to an international audience and to those who work on international programmes and projects.

Environmental context ∎

Issues of financial management cannot be considered in isolation from the environmental context in which they are located. That context will have both an external and an internal dimension. Indeed, it is the changing external context that has influenced changes in resource allocation methodology at both a national and an institutional level. To understand the rationale behind systems of resource allocation and financial management it will therefore be necessary to spend some time in a later chapter exploring the environmental context. Bligh *et al.* (1999) identified five ages in the making of the modern system of higher education:

1 The age of government support and the 'buffer principle'.
2 The age of expansion in the immediate post-war years.
3 The age of equality from the mid-1960s.
4 The age of efficiency from the mid-1970s.
5 The age of excellence from the late 1980s.

We shall here condense these periods into relative stability in funding, growth in turbulence, and continuing constraint. Each has been characterized by a different relationship between government and institutions. This has been reflected in different approaches to the allocation of resources and underlines the fact that there is a political as well as a technical dimension to the process. The relationship between political objectives and resource allocation methodology is explored in some depth in later chapters. For the present, however, it will be sufficient to remind ourselves of a few of the recent trends which have conditioned institutional responses to financial management. Those trends at a national level may be summarized as follows:

• There has been a move from an elite to a mass system of higher education. The percentage of the age group entering higher education in 2000 is over 30 per cent (higher in Scotland), twice that of the early 1990s. This has changed the profile of students, who now have wider entry qualifications and age range, a more diverse social background and demand more flexible degree structures and methods of learning (see Gledhill 1999). This has placed pressure on institutions to review course structures, teaching methods and modes of study and to invest in new technology to aid the learning process.
• The perceived focus of higher education has shifted towards meeting the economic and social demands of the nation rather than focusing primarily on the benefit to the individual. This raises a tension between what can be the short-term objectives of government and employers and the longer-term horizons of higher education. What is noticeable, however, is that the system has been subject to increasing external influence, most notably, perhaps, from government, employers, lay members of council and boards

of governors, and students themselves. In terms of the balance between institutional autonomy and public accountability, the pendulum has been swinging towards the latter.

- Government funding per student has been declining. The concept of 'efficiency gains' has focused attention on efficient and effective use of available resources and put a premium on the need to raise non-government income.
- Student grants have been replaced by loans and student fees have been introduced. As a consequence, students' attitudes are changing towards a more customer-orientated approach. Knowledge is becoming a commodity to be sold in the marketplace.
- The disappearance of the binary line as a consequence of the Further and Higher Education Act 1992 has increased the number of institutions with the title of university to over one hundred. This has increased competition between institutions, both for good students and for funding. It has also brought about a more diverse system and yet, as we explore in a later chapter, national funding methodology may not in fact be encouraging such diversity.
- Since the mid-1980s national funding mechanisms have moved towards using student numbers as a basis for teaching allocations and quality assessments for the funding of research. Selectivity in funding and the link between funding and quality have thereby increased. This linkage has affected institutional and individual behaviour patterns in the internal process of allocating resources.

Although the book is based on experience within the higher education sector, these trends and the issues they raise are not dissimilar to those encountered elsewhere in the education service, some might say in the public service as a whole. At a strategic level, decline in government funding, value for money and relevance to the economy are all phrases that will be familiar. Even the approaches of enhanced devolution to budget centres and formula-based approaches to resource allocation, accompanied by the rhetoric of efficiency and effectiveness, have been consistent between sectors. It is not surprising, therefore, that the issues addressed in the following pages are likely to be familiar to institutional managers in different parts of the education service, and, indeed, elsewhere in the public sector.

Institutional context ■

As a consequence of these national trends, institutional policies, practices and behavioural patterns have changed over time. Whilst the book aims to provide a guide to the management of financial resources, educational institutions are such complex institutions with such a range of cultures, practices and personalities that rarely would it be wise to advocate any one solution. It is worth remembering that organizations:

> are as different and varied as the nations and societies of the world. They have different cultures – sets of values and norms and beliefs – reflected in different structures and systems. And the cultures are affected by the events of the past and by the climate of the present, by the technology of the type of work, by their aims and the kind of people that work in them.
>
> (Handy 1993: 180)

Nevertheless, in response to the external environment there are a number of trends that are discernible at an institutional level. These may be summarized as follows:

- A change in culture away from collegial and sometimes bureaucratic styles towards the cultures of corporation and enterprise (see Watson 2000). There is, however, a tension in these developments. As McNay (1995a) and Davies (1987), for instance, have observed, the need for institutions to encourage income generation to compensate for decline in government funding implies an enterprise culture with freedom for individuals and groups to respond locally to initiatives and opportunities. The need for cost control and restructuring, however, implies a corporation culture in which both policy and operational detail are tightly controlled from the centre.
- A wider range of staff involved in financial management, particularly in the academic area, with deans and heads of department being expected to assume a more managerial role in addition to their traditional role of academic leadership.
- Devolution of budgetary responsibility to a departmental, faculty or school level, often incorporating within defined parameters the ability to transfer funds between budget heads and to carry forward surpluses and deficits from one year to the next.
- An increase in formulaic approaches to the allocation of resources, often incorporating to a greater or lesser extent a methodology that reflects that of the external funding agency.
- A shift in the performance indicators used to assess departments towards those of a financial nature.
- An increase in the management of academic activities at a departmental level to focus the efforts of the department and individual

members on areas in which they can best contribute to the financial health of the department. Thus, staff with a flourishing research programme are encouraged to pursue these activities to enhance research funding whilst less research-active colleagues are asked to undertake a correspondingly higher share of teaching.
• The development of marketing strategies on the basis of business plans to address the competitive environment.
• A change in the structure and roles of administrative departments with an increase in specialist staff and staff located in faculties, schools or departments.

There is always a danger that these trends may hide the fact that resource allocation schemes are not ends in themselves. The primary objective of the institution will remain excellence in teaching, research and other academic-related activities as defined in its mission statement and strategic objectives. Clearly, academic objectives will not be met unless the institution has a sound financial basis on which to operate, but the design and implementation of resource allocation methodologies need to be sensitive to the demands being placed on academic staff.

Resource allocation schemes and methods of financial management are tools for use by institutional managers in their search to ensure efficient and effective management of resources. They are not, however, merely technical instruments. They can also be used by senior managers to change the culture of an institution. Indeed, even in cases where such an intention is not a primary motive for implementing changes in procedures, the effect of certain resource allocation approaches can have the effect of impinging on the power structure of an institution with consequential effects on the underlying culture (see Dopson and McNay, chapter 2 in Warner and Palfreyman 1996).

From the above summaries of the environmental and institutional contexts it is evident that the task of managing financial resources will need to take account of internal and external considerations and both technical and behavioural issues. Clearly, there will be technical issues to discuss, such as:

• the influence of the external environment on internal mechanisms;
• the concepts of devolution and formula-based systems;
• the relationship between the planning process, the allocation of resources and the budgetary process.

Equally important, however, will be a range of behavioural issues such as:

- the preferences, priorities, skills and experience of the various staff involved in the process;
- the training and development of those staff;
- the use, availability and sophistication of appropriate technology (see Elkin and Law 2000);
- the history and culture of the institution; and
- the micropolitical climate in which the process is operating.

International context

Whilst the above sections have referred specifically to the UK context, issues surrounding financial management and resource allocation are international in scope. As a consequence, many of the themes observable within the UK can also be seen in other countries, albeit with local variations.

If we take, for instance, the balance between institutional autonomy and public accountability, the shift in the UK and many western countries has been towards an increase in government intervention and influence. In central and eastern Europe, on the other hand, the post-communist era has seen a move towards decentralization from government to institutions. Both these trends have placed additional financial responsibilities on institutional managers at a time when government funding for institutions is limited. As a consequence, a key issue for institutional managers is the efficient and effective use of resources.

Interestingly, despite the different historical backgrounds, the response to these challenges has had three similar features:

1 There has been a focus on the relationship between strategic planning and the effective use of resources. In the UK, for instance, it is often the case that effective management of resources is seen as being dependent upon deans and heads of department accepting a greater degree of responsibility for the financial health of the institution. The central administration, it is argued, is not in as good a position to respond to the external environment as staff working at the interface between the internal and external environment. The central European position, however, has historically been one of funding directly from government to faculties. It is the central authorities of the institution that have been weak in terms of institutional planning and financial management expertise. With decentralization from government to institutions as a priority in the post-communist world, effective institutional management is increasingly being seen as dependent upon a

strengthening of the institutional planning process. This implies a more authoritative role for staff working at an institutional level.

2 Perhaps linked with a desire to strengthen the strategic planning process, there has been a move towards funding systems that have a rational basis for institutional allocations. The shift in the UK towards formulaic funding has been mentioned above, but it has also been noticeable that, in countries emerging from Soviet domination, governments have been looking towards the adoption of formulaic approaches, based largely on student numbers, as a way of allocating resources to institutions rather than indulging in an annual bidding process.

3 Structures of governance have come under review. In the UK since the mid-1980s, lay governors have been encouraged to take a more active role in the governance of their institutions. The period has seen, for instance, the emergence of planning committees with both academic and lay members reflecting a breakdown in the old divisions between academic and business activities of the institution. Similarly, with pressure for accountability, systems of governance in central and eastern Europe that have traditionally relied exclusively upon academic membership have come under pressure to establish governing bodies that include representation from social partners.

Internationally, therefore, there have emerged during the 1980s and 1990s common pressures, increasingly common responses, and consequences that have implications for the appointment, training and development of a range of staff involved in the management of financial resources. In exploring these issues, it is hoped that the book might be a useful reference not just for UK readers but also for those in other countries who, albeit with different cultures and traditions, are facing many similar issues.

Structure of the book ▪

Following this introductory chapter, the book consists of eight further chapters and a bibliography. Chapter 2, which is intended as a background to the more detailed chapters to follow, surveys the changing environmental context incorporating government policy, declining resources, changes in national funding methodology, devolution and demands for public accountability. In particular, there is a focus on developments during the 1980s and 1990s leading to pressures for more efficient and effective management of resources at a time of financial constraint. The adoption by the funding agency of a more transparent and formula-based methodology and the influence of the Jarratt Report (1985) in recommending enhanced devolution to budget centres will be seen as significant catalysts for change. Chapter 3 briefly reviews institutional responses to the changing environment. A range of current issues is identified and some of the underlying factors that contribute to an understanding of them will be explored. Although the book is intended as a practical guide, the chapter includes reference to some theoretical literature in order to provide a few frameworks for understanding some of the key issues. These may help to explain how and why approaches have changed over time. They may also help to explain what has occasionally gone wrong and might give some guidance on the pitfalls to be avoided. Chapter 3 concludes by outlining a three-stage approach to the allocation of resources covering:

1 the need for institutions to understand their income streams, whether emanating from government, funding councils, research councils, students or elsewhere;
2 the need for institutions to apply strategic considerations and managerial judgement before allocating funds to their constituent parts; and
3 the process by which funds are allocated internally to departments, schools or faculties.

Each of Chapters 4 to 6 explores one of these stages. Chapter 4 explains the background to various sources of income, including the government's public expenditure round, the role of the higher education funding councils (HEFCs) and their methodology for allocating institutional grant. The components of that grant are explained, but the temptation to describe at length current HEFCs' funding methodology is resisted as far as possible, although some detail will be given by way of illustration. What is more important is the need to understand the principles behind the ways in which institutions gain their funding. The consequences of a shift towards a higher contribution from students is also explored.

The thrust of Chapter 5 will be on the need to reflect internal priorities in determining allocations to different sections of the institution. Internal and external considerations are considered and reference made to different models to meet strategic objectives. The chapter explores the link between the management of financial resources and the process of strategic planning. These processes are seen in terms of an annual cycle incorporating strategic planning, resource allocation, budgeting and monitoring, the omission of any part of which is likely to impair the whole process. This concept is important because, as resource allocation mechanisms have become more transparent and formulaic, the link has become greater between a department's performance in terms of attracting funds and the amount of money allocated by the institution to individual departments. For departments with income-generating potential this is an attractive proposition, but it may not necessarily be to the long-term advantage of the institution as a whole. The strategic planning process, therefore, needs to maintain a balance between creating incentives for established departments and creating the potential to fund new initiatives for the benefit of the institution. Chapter 5 reviews current pressures and some of the reasons for wishing to resist them.

Having prevailed upon the reader to grasp the importance of taking account of strategic considerations, Chapter 6 reviews mechanisms for determining the basis of allocating funds to the constituent parts of an organization. Again, the temptation to analyse in detail some of the formulaic approaches adopted by institutions is resisted, but it is in this chapter that the concepts of devolution and formulaic approaches are considered. No one system, however, is likely to be suitable for all institutions as many different factors will need to be taken into account. It is in this chapter that these factors are considered, including staffing issues, information systems and organizational characteristics.

Having reviewed the various phases of the resource allocation process, Brian Lewis, in Chapter 7, focuses attention on the need for the monitoring of expenditure, reviewing the external regulatory framework and the requirements for internal control. Recent initiatives to promote good practice are reviewed, including space management and issues of costing and pricing. Although it is not the intention here to delve into the intricacies of accounting practice, there are certain accounting issues that need to be widely understood, particularly in the context of devolved budgeting. Issues such as commitment accounting, the charging for central services, the carry forward of surpluses and deficits, and the treatment of capital expenditure are discussed. A final section reviews the changing role of the finance office.

In many respects the foregoing chapters will be seen as having assumed the perspective of senior managers operating within the central administration of the institution. Issues of resource allocation and financial management, however, are equally important at a faculty, school and departmental level and many of the issues already discussed will be equally applicable at that level. Not only will decisions of senior management impact at this level, but also institutions are increasingly dependent upon the income-generating activities of academic staff. This implies an entrepreneurial attitude on the part of staff, and inevitably that has had an impact on the management of departments. Increasingly, too, the ability to attract income, whether from governmental or non-governmental sources is being linked with assessment of quality. The impact of the research assessment exercise (RAE) is an obvious example. This in turn has added further management burdens at a departmental level. In Chapter 8, Peter Hodson joins me in addressing some of these issues from a departmental perspective. The chapter reviews in particular the changing role of the head of department, academic staffing issues and strategic considerations.

A final chapter pulls together various themes that run through previous chapters. These include institutional culture, concepts of power, staff training and development, management information systems, structural issues and the management of change. The chapter concludes with a few observations on the implications for institutional managers.

Further reading

See especially the related volumes in the Managing Universities and Colleges series:

- On the management of higher education institutions generally: Warner and Palfreyman 1996.
- On the legal context within which higher education institutions operate: Palfreyman and Warner 1998.
- On the state of UK higher education: Warner and Palfreyman 2001.
- On strategic management: Watson 2000.
- On information systems: Elkin and Law 2000.
- On the academic unit: Bolton 2000.

2

ENVIRONMENTAL CONTEXT

Introduction

This chapter aims to provide an outline of developments and trends in the management of financial resources in the context of external pressures. It will trace the changing nature of government policy and the role of the funding bodies and will place in context the major catalysts for change that have influenced management practices.

It is always difficult to know where to start an historical review. For the purposes of gaining an insight into current issues, it is developments over the decades of the 1980s and 1990s that are the most relevant. It is on those that we shall concentrate most. There is a danger, however, in ignoring earlier periods. Although it is inconceivable that life will return to what some will view as halcyon days, the present is always conditioned by the past. Whilst education institutions are now staffed with 'Thatcher's children', there was, after all, life before the infamous government cuts of 1981. Whatever may be the view of politicians and others on the efficiency and effectiveness of institutions in the pre-Thatcher period, it is worth remembering that British higher education had an international reputation for the quality of its teaching and research. Resource allocation and methods of financial management are primarily techniques to underpin the objectives associated with academic excellence. Presumably, therefore, within the prescriptions of the time, the management techniques being employed were consistent with the demands of the system and the priorities of individual institutions. We therefore briefly delve into what some will see as a prehistoric age in order to understand some of the principles underlying the process of managing financial resources during that period. This might also help to understand some of the later changes in approach and the pressures that influenced decisions on resource allocation methodology.

A touch of prehistory ■

The history of public funding of the universities has been extensively documented. For those who wish for further reading, a selection of texts is given in the bibliography. Some of these texts focus on the relationship between higher education and the state (Berdahl 1957; Barnes 1973; Carswell 1985; Booth 1987) some specifically on the role of the University Grants Committee (UGC) (Owen 1980; Shattock and Berdahl 1985; Shinn 1986), whilst others look more specifically at funding arrangements during the 1980s (Moore 1987; Clayton 1988a,b; Shattock 1992). There are also interesting international comparative works that include funding arrangements and the relationship between institutions and the state (Mauch and Sabloff 1995; Ziderman and Albrecht 1995; Henkel and Little 1999; Teather 1999).

The first government grant to the university colleges was in 1889. Various committees were established to advise on the allocations until, in 1919, the UGC was established by a Treasury minute. The terms of reference of the UGC were: 'to enquire into the financial needs of university education in the United Kingdom and to advise the Government as to the application of any grants that may be made by Parliament towards meeting them'.

It is evident, therefore, that at this stage the focus of the UGC was on advice to government rather than on direction to institutions. These terms of reference were subsequently expanded to incorporate a responsibility:

to collect, examine and make available information on matters relating to university education throughout the United Kingdom; and to assist, in consultation with the universities and other bodies concerned, the preparation and execution of such plans for the development of the universities as may from time to time be required *in order that they are fully adequate to national needs.*

(emphasis added)

With these terms of reference it is easy to understand how the UGC came to be seen as a 'buffer' between the government and universities.

Given recent emphasis on the need for institutions to raise non-government income, it is worth commenting that, as late as 1939, universities received only one-third of their income from the state. It is also noticeable that even in the early days of the UGC the government was seeing universities in terms of meeting national need.

Dawn of the modern age ∎

Looking at the history of the UGC, two things first happened in the early 1960s that are taken for granted today:

1 the funding requested by the UGC for the universities was reduced by government, and
2 the understanding that universities could use their grants more-or-less as they thought fit became subject increasingly to firm guidelines issued by the UGC.

These changes reflected the changing environment. The post-war period had been one of expansion in student numbers, an expansion that was sustained by the Robbins Report (Robbins 1963). The Robbins principle that, 'courses of higher education should be available for all those who are qualified by ability and attainment to pursue them and who wish to do so', dominated subsequent higher education thinking. In the years to come, however, the concept that student places should be determined according to student demand placed an increasing burden on the Treasury. This was particularly so since the Anderson Report (1960) had led to the introduction of mandatory grants for subsequent generations of students. The Treasury was faced with an open-ended commitment. It is not surprising that it and the UGC become more directive.

The 1960s also saw the birth of the binary system, with the upgrading or merging of some non-university institutions to form polytechnics. This sector was to be more vocationally and teaching orientated and more locally based than the universities. There was an implication that universities had not been sufficiently responsive to national needs. This sector was also to be subject to more direct government financial control. Independence in terms of its planning horizons was also restricted. Whereas the universities operated on a five-year planning horizon that had enabled them to plan for the future with a reasonable degree of certainty, there was to be no such quinquennial system for public sector institutions. Polytechnics were to be subject to one-year budgets and to the constraints of their local education authority's financial and staffing policies.

Many of the professional administrative and managerial functions exercised within universities did not develop within polytechnics until after the granting of corporate status following the Education Reform Act 1988.

There is one other notable event of the 1960s that demonstrates the concern about the increasing cost of higher education. In 1969, Shirley Williams, the minister for higher education, asked universities to consider what became known as the 'thirteen points' to reduce escalating costs. The ideas included, for instance, the reduction of student grants and the institution of loans. Compared with what was to follow, the tone of the approach was remarkably consultative, but it was perhaps indicative of an age that had already passed that the university sector remained unresponsive. Many of the thirteen points have now been put into practice.

Concerns at escalating costs were converted into action during the 1970s. The decade was one of high inflation. It commenced with increasing student numbers but, from the middle of the decade, student numbers in public sector institutions were reduced although those in the universities continued to increase slowly. Beneath an apparent increase in funding for institutions lay an actual reduction in the amount of government funding per student: a decline that was to continue. Under inflationary pressure, the quinquennial system broke down in 1975. In 1979, government withdrew its funding for overseas students leading to the charging of full-cost fees.

Reflections

Before moving to the more modern period it is worthwhile to pause and consider the distinctive features that are discernible in the process of managing financial resources at this time. They may, perhaps, be summarized as follows:

- When the university sector was small in terms of numbers of students and institutions and receiving a minority of its funds from the state, government showed little inclination to interfere in its operation.
- The consequences of expansion were slow to be appreciated. The combination of student expansion fuelled by the Robbins Report (1963) and mandatory grants implemented after the Anderson Report (1960) created a financial commitment and expectation that were likely to be unsustainable in the long term.
- Government realization at the size of the commitment led to a desire for greater central control in terms of curricula and finance

as witnessed by the orientation and funding mechanisms associated with the establishment of the polytechnics.

- Universities were themselves slow to react to a changing world. Shirley Williams's thirteen points represented a look into the future. The response of the university sector looked back to a previous golden age of state-funded expansion.
- As the government's financial commitment increased and inflation raged, policy directives turned into more detailed practical intervention. UGC 'guidance' increased, full-cost fees were introduced for overseas students and the quinquennial system of planning for universities was abandoned.

So far the discussion has tended to involve issues at the system level of higher education, but are there any particular characteristics of institutional management that can be detected during this period? It is always dangerous to generalize, but perhaps it is safe to say that compared to the late 1990s:

- institutions were smaller in size;
- the culture of institutions tended to be more collegial;
- academic staff could focus on their academic activities safe within the concept of tenure, providing lifetime security of employment and without undue regard for the financial situation of their institution;
- universities considered teaching and research to be interrelated activities with a single institutional grant from the UGC covering both activities;
- deans and heads of department were regarded as academic leaders appointed primarily on the basis of their academic credentials;
- the range of management functions to be performed was more restricted and less complex; and
- the number of persons employed as university administrators was initially small but grew from the mid-1960s with a recognition of the need for professional skills in a wider range of managerial activities.

The development in the role of the professional, career administrator is well captured in the title of a collection of essays to mark the silver jubilee of the Conference of University Administrators: *Beyond the Limelight* (Bosworth 1986). The history of this body reflects the growth in size and complexity of institutional management of which managing financial resources is an important part. The first Meeting of University Academic Administrative Staffs (MUAAS) took place with 12 people on 16 September 1961. The title reflected the origins of the organization. It had grown from the initiative of staff in the University of Manchester working in the area of academic administration. By the early 1970s, however, the title was an anachronism. Those attending the annual conference worked in a range of areas, including finance offices. In 1973, these changes were reflected in a new title: Conference of University Administrators (CUA). Some 450 participants attended the first CUA annual conference in 1974. By comparison, over 1000 participants attended the annual meeting of the Association of University Administrators (AUA) formed in 1993 by the amalgamation of CUA and APA (Association of Polytechnic Administrators). The annual conference now represents only a small part of the services provided for a membership that had reached over 3700 by the year 2000. Those services include its own international journal, *perspectives: Policy and Practice in Higher Education.*

The modern age

The cuts of 1981

If we return now to the narrative of events, an appropriate point to commence a discussion of the modern age is 1979, the year in which a Conservative government was returned to power. It has been argued, for instance by Allen (1988), that the government did not have a policy on the universities as such until the publication in 1985 of its Green Paper on higher education entitled *The Development of Higher Education into the 1990s* (DES 1985). It did, however, have a firm commitment to reduce public expenditure, and this was applied to the universities in 1981. There had been some mild foretaste of things to come: the quinquennial system had been abandoned in 1975 and fees for overseas students had been introduced in 1979, but 1981 was the year that will go down in history as marking a dramatic change in government policy towards the universities.

Responsibility for implementing the cuts rested with the UGC. This placed the UGC in a dilemma. Rather than being the interface or buffer between universities and government it was now clearly the implementer of government policy. There were some who took the view that the UGC should refuse to be associated with this change of approach. The view prevailed, however, that government policy would not be changed by such a refusal and universities themselves would be worse off without the involvement of the UGC with its understanding of the university system.

The approach adopted by the UGC was to try as far as possible to protect the unit of resource by reducing student numbers. It planned for a reduction in student numbers between 1979/80 and 1983/84 of between 3 and 5 per cent and an average worsening of about 10 per cent in the unit of resource. This represented a possible retreat from the Robbins principle that 'courses of higher education should be available for all those who are qualified by ability and attainment to pursue them and who wish to do so'. The demand for higher education, however, was met by expansion in the polytechnics. As a consequence, the government, in its Green Paper of 1985, was able to claim that: 'there has continued in practice to be a place somewhere in higher education for all those qualified and seeking to enter' (DES 1985: para. 3.1).

The UGC also had to decide on how reductions would be shared between institutions. The choice was between 'equal misery' and 'differential cuts'. The same dilemma faced vice-chancellors and institutions when grants were announced. The approach adopted by the UGC, as it was subsequently by many vice-chancellors, was to opt for differential cuts. As a consequence, the size and impact of the cuts differed between universities. The average was about 15 per cent, but for some institutions it reached 40 per cent. The basis of the decision-making process was unclear, but there was a suspicion that the size of cut was influenced by the UGC's perception of the quality of the student intake. The lack of detailed explanation again reflects the style of the age.

The way in which institutions responded to their reduced grants can also be seen as marking the passing from one age to the next. Institutions with cuts approaching the 40 per cent level were faced with devising strategies for survival. Income-generating activity, reduction of costs and a fundamental refocusing of activities were all employed.

Even in institutions with reductions in grant at about the average level, the dramatic nature of the cuts forced changes in approach. Perhaps at least three changes can be observed from this period:

First, there was an increased focus on institutional plans. Often these were written by the vice-chancellor with varying degrees of consultation with senior colleagues. Those who were most successful ensured that they had the support of influential members of senate before the plans were submitted. Sometimes plans were initially defeated by senate and had to be resubmitted. Their resubmission often involved a higher degree of lobbying and gaining of support rather than a fundamental reappraisal of the proposals.

Second, these plans often adopted the approach of 'differential cuts' rather than 'equal misery' compared with earlier organic growth.

Except in a few cases, it may still be too early to say that institutions were defining their objectives in terms of mission statements. The immediate pressure was focused on how to make rapid savings, but inevitably that forced a definition of priority areas.

Third, an increase in the use of integrated data for planning purposes. What had hit the universities was a financial crisis, but the response often reflected an age in which planning had been undertaken in an academic forum. Staff/student ratios were perhaps the most popular measure of comparing departments. In at least some institutions, the financial crisis was now converted into academic terms by calculating how far staff/student ratios would have to worsen. Not all staff cost the same, however, and when departments submitted projected staff savings in terms of posts these did not necessarily amount to the level of financial savings required. Clearly, planning could no longer be seen entirely in academic terms. Financial indicators such as unit costs and income and expenditure statements for each department would have to be given a higher profile. For many institutions, perhaps inevitably given the time constraints, the emphasis remained on cost reduction. Income generation was seen in terms of a long-term objective dependent upon central university initiatives rather than as a priority for departmental staff.

Post-1981

In the aftermath of the 1981 cuts, the government asked the UGC for advice on the development of a strategy for higher education into the 1990s. The secretary of state was Sir Keith Joseph and the tone of the consultation process reinforced the change in the nature of the relationship between government, UGC and universities. The letters from government were clearly written from master to servant. Planning for an age of declining government resources had also arrived, although it was still not recognized as a long-term environmental factor. Having consulted widely, the UGC submitted its advice in *A Strategy for Higher Education into the 1990s*, published in September 1984 (UGC 1984). At the same time, a similar document was published by the National Advisory Body for Local Authority Higher Education (NAB) which had also been approached by government as part of the review process (NAB 1984).

In terms of allocating resources, the UGC's response drew a clear break with past policies. It announced its intention 'to develop a more systematic and selective approach to our allocation of funds for research' (UGC 1984: para. 5.2). It also gave a boost to the establishment of priorities and the formulation of planning statements within universities. Its own strategy, it said, would 'not be effective unless the universities make a complementary effort to develop explicit research strategies and improve their management' (para. 5.2), and it encouraged rationalization by announcing that, 'in allocating funds we shall discriminate in favour of universities which tackle the problem of small departments' (para. 10.5).

Whilst such statements were consistent with government philosophy and an emerging managerialist approach, the UGC represented the strong views of institutions when it pressed the government to provide, at a minimum, 'truly level funding of recurrent grant at least until the end of the decade' (para. 8.6); to introduce a longer planning horizon (para. 8.21); and to make 'an explicit statement revoking the principle of deficiency funding so as to encourage universities and potential donors' (para. 9.9).

The government's response was contained in its Green Paper, *The Development of Higher Education into the 1990s*, published in May 1985 (DES 1985). A number of points can be highlighted which set the tone of higher education for succeeding years and influenced changes in resource allocation methodology at a national and institutional level. These may be summarized as follows:

- The emphasis of higher education was shifting away from serving the needs of the individual towards the needs of the nation. The government stressed its belief 'that it is vital for our higher education to contribute more effectively to the improvement of the performance of the economy' (para. 1.2). There was, the government believed, 'continuing concern that higher education does not always respond sufficiently to changing economic needs' (para. 2.2). In future, 'the Universities in particular need to develop greater ability to adapt to change' (para. 1.5).
- This led to comments on subject balance in higher education. The government 'believes it right to maintain a distinct emphasis on technological and directly vocational courses' (para. 2.9), whilst 'arts provision should to some extent be concentrated in the interests of cost-effectiveness' (para. 2.11). Additional funds were made available by government to address concerns at the inadequate supply of high quality, skilled graduates in the fields of electronic engineering, computer science and related disciplines.
- The fundamental belief in the interrelationship of teaching and research was challenged as a sacred cow of UK higher education. The government maintained that, 'there is no evidence that all academic staff must engage in research' (para. 5.4).
- Higher education establishments were to be expected to develop increased links with industry and commerce and with local

communities in general (para. 1.6). Institutions were expected to seek closer links with employers, 'which are essential if higher education is to realise its full potential in meeting the needs of the economy' (para. 2.3).

This vision of the future of higher education underpinned comments on funding issues, in particular:

- The UGC's plea for level funding was clearly not part of the government's thinking. It was anticipated that there would be a requirement for 'continuing gains in efficiency across higher education if standards are to be maintained, entailing rationalisation of provision and selectivity in the application of the resources available' (para. 9.3).
- In the longer term, the government foresaw not only rationalization within institutions but also the amalgamation or closure of whole institutions (para. 9.9).
- Whilst it was recognized that reliance on public finance was to a great extent unavoidable, the government wished to see it reduced, with an increase in funding from non-government sources. To this end it confirmed, 'that increases in income from outside sources will not lead to reductions in Government funding' (para. 1.9).
- The government emphasized the need to increase the effectiveness of the money spent on research which 'requires concentration in strong centres . . . An important thrust of research policy over the next few years will be towards selectivity and concentration' (para. 1.11) such that some departments or even whole universities might lose research funding from the UGC (para. 5.7).

The Green Paper was, of course, a disappointment to the higher education sector, particularly the prospect of a continuing decline in resources in real terms. On selectivity of research funding, the Green Paper had gone further than the UGC was intending to do. Although the UGC confirmed that it would be markedly more selective than before in the allocation of resources, it envisaged that each university's grant would include a basic allowance for research.

UGC's funding methodology

The UGC's new approach to the distribution of resources was first used for the distribution of recurrent grant for the academic year 1986/87. Funding for teaching was to be determined according to student numbers planned and agreed for 1989/90 and a unit of resource that differed between subjects (cost centres) but not between institutions. Funding for research was to be selective with both quantitative and qualitative criteria and based on the results of a research selectivity exercise. The various components of the model were as follows:

T   Resources to be distributed on teaching-based criteria in proportion to each university's share of the planned student load for the cost centre. The load was weighted for undergraduates, taught postgraduates and research postgraduates.

R   Resources to be distributed on research-based criteria using four components:

    DR   relating to income from research councils and charitable bodies;

    CR   relating to contract research income;

    SR   relating to staff and research student numbers (this was the 'floor' provision for research); and

    JR   resources selectively distributed on the basis of the research assessment exercise. The balance between SR and JR could vary between cost centres.

S   Resources for special factors divided between:

    NDS   non-departmental special factors; and

    DS   departmental special factors.

The UGC emphasized that, 'although the approach and procedures are new, the outcome is a block grant, as before. Responsibility for deciding how the grant should be spent continues to rest with institutions in the light of their own circumstances and of any guidance which the Committee may provide' (UGC, 1986: para. 3). Accordingly the UGC intended not to publish details of the coefficients in its formula: 'Since these figures are averages for Great Britain as a whole they are of limited relevance to individual institutions for internal resource allocation' (para. 20). Many institutional managers, however, did not share this view. Encouraged by the Jarratt Report (see below) to adopt more quantitative approaches based on principles of cost centre accounting, the UGC's calculations provided a ready starting point for the development of internal resource allocation models. Although the UGC had not divulged the details of its formula, there were sufficient indications of approach and sufficient published data for institutions to undertake their own interpretation of how their grant had been calculated.

These developments prompted the view that, 'by 1985, the UGC had become a full-blooded planning organization which required universities to respond in the same mode' (Becher and Kogan 1992: 45). This new approach by the UGC was one of the two primary catalysts for change in institutional management practices.

Jarratt Report

The second major catalyst for change was the Jarratt Report, published in March 1985. The Jarratt Committee was appointed 'to promote and co-ordinate . . . a series of efficiency studies of the management of the universities concerned' (para. 1), a task judged by the Committee as being 'to examine whether management structure and systems were effective in ensuring that decisions are fully informed, that optimum value is obtained from the use of resources, that policy objectives are clear, and that accountabilities are clear and monitored' (para. 1.2).

The Jarratt Committee expressed the view that it was 'in the planning and use of resources that universities have the greatest opportunity to improve their efficiency and effectiveness' (para. 3.27). In an assessment of its findings, the Committee commented that, 'in some universities there is still a strong emphasis on maintaining the historical distribution of resources. Planning and resource allocation tend to be incremental rather than dynamic. Mechanisms and procedures which were suitable for growth have been retained in quite different circumstances' (para. 3.40). The report continued by stating that:

> among the reasons for this are the strong forces within each university. They include large and powerful academic departments together with individual academics who sometimes see their academic discipline as more important than the long-term well-being of the university which houses them. We stress that in our view universities are first and foremost corporate enterprises to which subsidiary units and individual academics are responsible and accountable.
>
> (para. 3.41)

In summary, the Committee urged that efficient and effective financial management in the new environment required universities:

- to establish planning and resources committees;
- to use more extensively performance indicators;
- to recognize the vice-chancellor as chief executive; and

- to devolve a greater degree of financial management to cost centres, with the objective 'to improve planning, to sharpen the allocation of resources and to ensure that budget setting carries appropriate tasks and pressures into budget centres' (para. 3.44).

Such comments challenged both the mechanics of resource allocation and the culture of institutions.

Not surprisingly, the Report has had its critics. It has been seen, for instance, as attempting 'to promote management into a self-justifying activity . . . [taking] on imperatives of its own' (Becher and Kogan 1992: 181), and as being 'explicitly hostile to the power of departments' with no mention of 'the functions of teachers, researchers or students' (ibid.: 47). Burrell (1993: 74) has seen the Jarratt Report as 'putting to an end any thoughts of a defence of an intellectual communitas by effectively reducing the power of the professional academic for the benefit of university administrators and "senior" professors'. Similarly, the Committee's view that 'universities are first and foremost corporate enterprises to which subsidiary units . . . are responsible and accountable' (para. 3.41) runs counter to the concept of the basic unit as being arguably a functional necessity in higher education (Becher and Kogan 1992). A great omission was seen to be 'in procedures relating to income generation, how you manage it, how you monitor it, how you provide incentives to departments, how you make internal investment decisions, how you assimilate new income streams into your resource allocation process' (Shattock 1986).

In summary, a view emerged that the Jarratt Report concentrated on the 'hard S's' of structure, strategy and systems and neglected the 'soft S's' of skills, style, shared-values and staff. There was seen to be a compensatory need to preach 'climate' and 'culture' rather than 'control' and 'confrontation' (Palfreyman 1989). Interestingly, whilst the Jarratt Committee was persuading universities to adopt a more managerialist approach, it was informal, interpersonal skills that were being seen as essential in the management of large corporations in the modern world: 'the informal conversations (not the formal, usually written, communication) provide the order in the organization' (Bergquist 1993: 138).

This tension between a central managerialist approach focusing on efficiency, effectiveness and cost saving and a more devolved, incentives-driven approach is one that has continued throughout the 1980s and 1990s and is an issue to which we return. For the present, it is sufficient to note that in the process of implementing new methods of resource allocation, institutions need to recognize the limitations of the Jarratt Report and to go beyond structure and systems and embrace concepts of culture and shared values: the managerialism–collegiality debate in UK higher education, corporatism–shared values in US higher education terms (see Tapper and Palfreyman, 1998, 2000: 10–13).

Continuing developments

The years 1985 and 1986 had seen the setting of the foundations of future models for distributing financial resources. The following year was to see a confirmation and consolidation of that process. In April 1987, the government's White Paper on higher education, subtitled *Meeting the Challenge* (DES 1987), stated that:

- the aims and purposes of higher education should be not only to 'pursue basic scientific research and scholarship in the arts and humanities' but also to 'serve the economy more effectively' and to 'have closer links with industry and commerce, and promote enterprise';
- means to improve quality would include 'more selectively funded research, targeted with attention to prospects for commercial exploitation';
- efficiency was to be increased by 'improvements in institutional management'; 'changes in the management of the system' and by 'the development and use of performance indicators'; and
- the UGC was to be reconstituted as a smaller, statutorily incorporated, Universities Funding Council (UFC) which would 'be responsible for the distribution of funds among universities in Great Britain under new contract arrangements'.

In May 1987, the theme of greater selectivity in research funding reappeared in a discussion document prepared by the Advisory Board for the Research Councils (ABRC) entitled *A Strategy for the Science Base* (ABRC 1987). The document reminded readers of earlier reports (Merrison 1982; Morris 1983) which had drawn attention to the rising real costs of experimental research and which had called for individual universities to concentrate research resources in selected areas and to establish administrative structures such as research committees to make this possible (para. 1.11). The ABRC report now recommended a future pattern of provision that envisaged three types of institution differentiated according to their range of research activity (para. 1.31). This differentiation did not materialize, although there became overtones of the idea in the way in which members of the Committee of Vice-Chancellors and Principals (CVCP) came to meet in different informal groups depending upon the nature of their institution.

Education Reform Act 1988

The most significant event of the period, however, was the passing of the Education Reform Act 1988 (DES 1988). That Act (ss 121–128), removed from local education authority (LEA) control the polytechnics and larger higher education colleges and institutes. These institutions were to be controlled by their own governing bodies and funded through a new agency, the Polytechnics and Colleges Funding Council (PCFC). The movement leading towards the abolition of the binary line had begun. The UGC was replaced by the UFC as envisaged in the earlier White Paper (DES 1987).

The Act also provides an important environmental context in that it introduced financial delegation to school governors and head teachers and provided for school budgets to be determined on a formula basis (ss 33–51). The government's purpose in introducing local management of schools (LMS) was stated as a way of improving the quality of teaching and learning in schools because it would:

1 enable governing bodies and head teachers of schools to plan their use of resources to maximum effect in accordance with their own needs and priorities; and
2 make schools more responsive to their clients: parents, pupils, the local community and employers.

These sentiments were replicated within higher education in the context of enhanced devolution of budgetary responsibility within institutions as advocated by the Jarratt Committee.

The period from the return of the Conservative government in 1979 to the passing of the Education Reform Act in 1988 has been considered in some detail for two reasons. First, it was a formative period in establishing a new methodology for the allocation of resources to institutions, and second, this new methodology, combined with pressure to adopt more managerialist approaches, forced institutions to review their own internal financial management practices. These are issues to which we return in later chapters.

Further and Higher Education Act 1992

Only three years after the Education Reform Act, a government White Paper, *Higher Education – A New Framework* (DES 1991), was proposing the abolition of the binary policy. The Further and Higher Education Act 1992 (DES 1992) enabled polytechnics and some colleges of higher education to gain university status. The UFC and PCFC were replaced by the Higher Education Funding Council for England (HEFCE) and similar bodies for Scotland and Wales. Northern Ireland, too, had its own arrangements. These newly formed funding councils were faced with the task of unifying the different funding methodologies prevailing before 1992 in the universities' and polytechnics' sectors.

The Act also placed a duty on the funding councils to develop wide-ranging systems of quality assessment. The period since 1992 has been marked by quality assessment visitations which, in the words of the Higher Education Quality Council (HEQC), 'rank teaching and learning in the various subject areas by institution as a basis for informing funding decisions' (HEQC 1994: 5). Unlike the funding methodology for research, however, there was no direct relationship, except in Scotland, between quality assessments of teaching and the level of funding, although there was always the threat that unsatisfactory grades could lead to the withdrawal of funding.

Consolidation

Throughout the late 1980s and 1990s, the funding methodology remained based on teaching and research criteria. Institutions witnessed a new openness on the part of the funding body. Whilst the UGC had not divulged the coefficients within its formula, the UFC and its successor bodies gave far more detail about their methodology. There were still historic factors incorporated in the model that had been based on subjective judgement and might be open to criticism (Johnston 1993), but at least institutions had more data on which to base their internal decisions. Changes in funding methodology, further decline in the unit of resource and increased selectivity in research funding forced some institutions to rethink their internal resource allocation methodology.

Funding for teaching

Funding for teaching continued to comprise two elements: the funding councils' grant, and tuition fees. Although the detail of the funding councils' methodology has been subject to periodic revision, the essential approach has continued to be based on student numbers. The methodology is discussed further in Chapter 4. The government's policy on tuition fees for full-time undergraduate students, however, has changed according to whether it has wished to expand or consolidate participation in higher education:

- During the period 1989 to 1992, the general emphasis was on growth in student numbers, but at a reduced cost per student. The approach adopted was to reward efficiency as judged by universities' performance in recruiting 'fees-only' UK and EU students (i.e. UK and EU students in excess of those for whom it received government funding). The response of universities was such that the government's student number targets for the year 2000 were exceeded well before the end of the decade.
- Consequently in the Autumn statement of 1993, the government announced that it wished to see a period of consolidation over the three years from 1994/95. Fee levels were reduced by 45 per cent between 1993/94 and 1994/95 to discourage the recruitment of UK and EU fees-only students. The open-ended nature of encouraging the recruitment of fees-only students who, like other students, were eligible for mandatory grants covering fees and a proportion of living expenses according to parental income, had always been of concern to the Treasury. As a further deterrent, institutions were allocated maximum aggregate student numbers (MASNs), with the threat of penalties for exceeding agreed figures.

The 1990s also saw a change in the contribution expected from full-time undergraduate students towards their studies. At the start of the decade, tuition fees were paid by local education authorities and living costs were supported by a means-tested grant. In 1990, top-up loans were introduced to supplement the means-tested grant which was frozen at its then current level. The loan element increased until loan and maximum grant were in equal proportion. As evidence quoted in the Dearing Report (1997) demonstrates, however, even the loan plus grant was insufficient to cover a student's expenditure. As a consequence, most students were having to work to make up the shortfall, were taking out commercial loans or were being subsidized by their parents.

By the mid-1990s, the debate was about whether maintenance grants should be replaced in their entirety by loans and whether students should be required to make a contribution to the cost of tuition. Having considered a range of options, the Dearing Committee (Dearing Report 1997) recommended the introduction of fees and the retention of grants. The government, however, decided to introduce means-tested fees but abolished grants. The issue remains hotly debated in the context of encouraging wider access to higher education and also in the context of constitutional reform in the UK, with enhanced devolution of responsibility, for some aspects of student provision, to constituent parts of the UK.

Funding for research

Funding for research continued the policy of increased selectivity. The results of the second research assessment exercise (RAE) announced by the UFC in 1989 (UFC 1989) were based on a five- rather than a four-point scale and were accompanied by a change in judgemental (JR) funding methodology. Whilst in the first RAE all departments received at least some funding for research, those in category 1 in the 1989 exercise received no funding.

The first two RAEs had applied only to the universities. The 1992 exercise was the first since the abolition of the binary line. It represented a continuing emphasis on selectivity but gave some encouragement to those departments in former polytechnics that displayed research potential. Consequently, the research component of institutional grants for 1993/94 was composed of: QR + DevR + CR where:

QR   was related to quality as measured by the research assessments and quantity as measured by the number of staff submitted for assessment.

DevR represented developmental funds to encourage research potential in institutions not within the previous UFC sector.

CR   was related to industrial and commercial contract income.

Ninety-five per cent (£585 million) of the funds available for research was allocated under QR. Compared with the original UGC methodology (see above), funding under DR had been transferred to the research councils and SR had been abolished with a shift towards staff rather than students as the volume measure within QR.

In 1994, as a further move towards enhanced accountability, the HEFCE indicated that, 'institutions should be required to report on their allocation of research funding' on an annual basis (HEFCE 1994: para. 12).

For the 1996 exercise, the five-point scale was expanded to a seven-point scale, selectivity was further increased, and the DevR component was abolished. Details are given in Chapter 4.

Conclusion   ■

This chapter has traced the development of government policy and the role of the UGC and its successor bodies. The Jarratt Report and the UGC's new resource allocation methodology were seen to be important catalysts for change. The purpose has been to give a

picture of the external environment which faced UK higher education institutions, particularly during the 1980s and 1990s. The 1980s
commenced with the dramatic and well-documented cuts of 1981 as
part of the government's policy of reducing public expenditure.
Thereafter, for the remainder of the millennium, there was a continuing decline in real terms in the unit of resource, accompanied
by demands for greater efficiency, accountability and selectivity.
Four charts taken from the Dearing Report (1997) summarize the
trends. Numbers of full-time UK students (Figure 2.1) and numbers
as a percentage of the 18–19 year old population (the age participation index) (Figure 2.2) have both been increasing. This growth has
been accompanied by real growth in total public expenditure on
higher education (Figure 2.3), but the level of public funding per
student (measured in constant prices) has fallen since at least 1976
(Figure 2.4).

An inevitable consequence was that demands on higher education
and its staff increased. Ironically, whilst moves towards a mass
system of higher education imply the need for a diversified system
catering for a wide range of institutions and clientele, funding
mechanisms have tended to encourage conformity of response at
an institutional level. It is to institutional issues that we turn in the
next chapter.

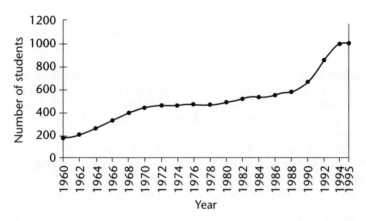

Figure 2.1 Full-time UK students in higher education in the UK
Source: DfEE
Notes: Numbers exclude Open University students who are regarded as being part-
time. Coverage is for publicly funded higher education only.
For the years 1960 to 1966 inclusive, an estimate of students from overseas has been
removed from published figures, which cover all students, to arrive at the figure for
home students. The figures for years 1994 and 1995 are provisional.

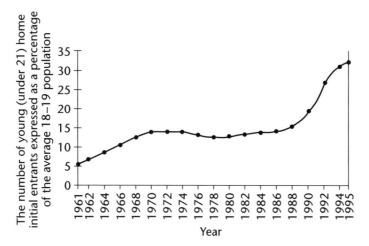

Figure 2.2 Higher education age participation index (API), GB institutions

Source: DfEE

Notes: Initial entrants are those entering a course of full-time higher education for the first time.

1961 figure estimated using Robbins Report App.2A, Table 3 (Percentage of the population of each age receiving higher education GB Oct 1961).

Due to minor change in definition, the years 1961 to 1970 inclusive are not strictly comparable with later years.

Due to minor change in definition, years from 1980 onwards are not strictly comparable with earlier years.

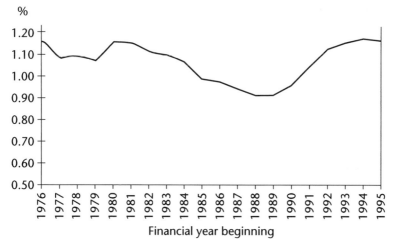

Figure 2.3 Public expenditure on higher education in the UK as a percentage of GDP

Source: DfEE

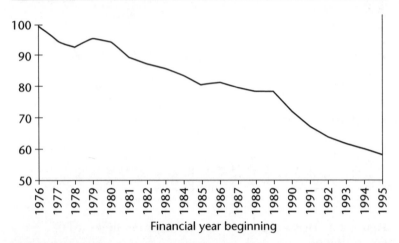

Figure 2.4   Index of public funding per student for higher education, 1976/77 to 1995/96
Source: DfEE

3

INSTITUTIONAL ISSUES

Introduction

The previous chapter provided a brief historical outline of the environmental context affecting the management of financial resources. It was seen that, in broad terms, the system has moved through a period of relative stability in funding, through a growth in turbulence, to a period of continuing financial constraint. In this chapter we begin by reviewing institutional responses to these three broad periods. This will help to explain how one system, that of the UK, came to be where it is, but we shall move rapidly to an identification of current issues facing institutions worldwide in the management of financial resources. The chapter continues by emphasizing that there is no single solution to these issues and that each institution will be governed in its response by a number of interrelated factors. These factors are then explored in general terms as a prelude to more detailed discussion in later chapters. To establish a framework for subsequent discussion, the chapter concludes by outlining a three-stage approach to the resource allocation process.

Historical review

Relative stability in funding

The period up to the mid-1970s was one of relative stability in terms of government funding. That is not to say that there were not profound changes within the higher education system during this time. Post-war expansion, the introduction of mandatory grants, the

Robbins Report, the expansion in the number and size of universities and the creation of the polytechnics were all significant landmarks which provided challenges for institutional managers. There was, however, certainly in comparison with what was to follow, an element of stability in funding arrangements. Generalizations are dangerous, but certain characteristics might be identified as being indicative of approaches to the management of financial resources in universities during this period, in particular:

• There was a clear differentiation between the role of senate and the role of council. Senate concerned itself with academic affairs and council with business activities including financial management.
• Strategic planning was conducted initially in terms of academic aspirations. Once these had been agreed by senate, the financial, staffing and space implications were considered by council.
• Institutional planning was dominated by the quinquennial system, although the polytechnics never had the luxury of such a planning horizon. Every five years there would be a large-scale planning exercise that might take anything up to two years to complete. Senate would approve academic plans for the next five years and council would approve resource plans in terms of staffing, space and finances to deliver the academic proposals. The quinquennial submission was then made to the UGC. These were substantial documents running to many pages of analysis and associated appendices
• There was an assumption that, once the university's plans had been approved by the UGC as part of the quinquennial planning exercise, there was a reasonable expectation that funding would be continued at the approved level during the quinquennium.
• There existed an almost paternalistic attitude to the internal allocation of resources. Heads of department and deans would fight their corner when seeking additional posts but their primary role was one of academic leadership.
• Financial management was something that happened within the central administration. Although heads of science-based departments would be involved in the management of research grants and contracts, departmental grants would be limited to relatively small sums required for recurrent expenditure.
• The annual allocation of resources was based in the main on bids from departments. Typically this might involved a number of separate processes:

  – Requests for additional academic staff or the filling of current vacancies. These would be submitted initially to a faculty committee.

This committee would prioritize the bids and submit them to a university committee that would approve those to be filled, primarily on the basis of the strength of the academic case in the light of available funding. Staff/student ratios were the primary performance indicator used for comparison between departments. Any correlation between the annual bids for posts and the plans submitted in the previous quinquennial statement was likely to be in the nature of a general understanding of the future direction of the institution rather than a direct comparison between annual bids and previously agreed long-term strategy.

– Requests for additional non-academic staff or the filling of current vacancies would be submitted by departments to a central university committee which might use some sort of formula, based on a ratio of academic to support staff, to determine the strength of submissions.

– A similar procedure was likely to be employed in respect of expenditure on equipment. The UGC made an equipment grant separate from its grant for teaching and research. This had to be spent on equipment, although additional equipment could be bought from the teaching and research grant.

– The annual departmental budget would be based on a submission to the vice-chancellor or a central university committee. It would be usual for a department to submit a 'wish list', knowing that whatever it submitted was likely to be reduced. There might be discussions between the department and staff in the finance office, but the final allocation was likely to be based on the size of the previous year's budget plus or minus a certain percentage depending upon the funds available for the university as a whole.

– It was not unusual for a new professor to be allowed a 'honeymoon period', during which time additional funds might be made available, usually on the authority of the vice-chancellor. The vice-chancellor might also have authority to approve certain pump-priming funds for strategic purposes.

– A central committee was likely to determine capital expenditure on buildings and the estate.

Growth in turbulence

The conditions of relative stability were shaken by the oil crisis of the mid-1970s. Inflation soared and the government could no longer provide five-year funding commitments. The quinquennial system came under pressure and was finally abandoned in 1975. There were hopes that suspension would be on a temporary basis and that longer-term planning periods would return. Any anticipation of a return to stability was short-lived. The consequences of the return of a Conservative government in 1979 are well documented and covered briefly in the previous chapter. Even so, there was hope that the cuts of 1981 would be a single event and that once the system had adjusted to the new level of funding a period of stability would return. That hope was fuelled by certain encouraging signs during 1984 and 1985, but they were to prove illusory. The period of declining resources had already begun, although many in institutions were still clinging to hopes of a return to a previous age. This should not be surprising. Senior members of staff who were being faced with the new external environment had gained their experience during a period of expansion and relative stability. Practices, procedures and attitudes developed during their earlier careers were bound to condition their response to the new environment. Nevertheless, the period saw the emergence of certain trends in the management of financial resources. These may be summarized as follows:

- A wider range of performance indicators was adopted.
- The planning process became more quantitative.
- Vice-chancellors took a lead in the development of strategies to cope with the changing circumstances.
- A greater awareness developed that there was a relationship between the rational and micro-political elements in the planning process.
- Heads of department became involved in matters of a more clearly financial nature.
- Planning shifted away from expansion to contraction.
- Cost saving took a higher profile than income generation on the grounds that it could have a more immediate effect.
- Income generation was seen as dependent upon university initiatives whereas cost savings were seen to operate at a departmental level.
- Financial management was centralized in the hands of the vice-chancellor, as the person linking the academic and business spheres of activity, and a few senior colleagues, particularly the finance officer.

Continuing constraint

Even if the period of declining resources had in reality begun some years earlier, the techniques associated with the new age began to take shape from the mid-1980s, spurred in particular by those two significant catalysts for change: the Jarratt Report (1985) and the

UGC's new funding methodology which took effect from the academic year 1986/87. These catalysts have been considered in some detail in the previous chapter, but it is worth summarizing the impact they had, and continue to have, on institutional approaches to the management of financial resources. Coming as they did within close proximity to each other, the UGC's methodology gave institutions the opportunity to implement some of the managerialist approaches urged on institutions by the Jarratt Committee. In particular, the Jarratt Report urged that efficient and effective financial management in the new environment required universities:

- to establish planning and resources committees;
- to establish a clearer relationship between the annual budget and a strategic plan;
- to use more extensively performance indicators;
- to recognize the vice-chancellor as chief executive;
- to place less reliance on the critical role of the vice-chancellor in the resource allocation process;
- to devolve a greater degree of financial management to cost centres; and
- to create more flexibility in the transfer of funds between heads of expenditure.

At the same time, the UGC's resource allocation methodology:

- broke with the historical pattern of allocations to institutions;
- was more open about its approach, although it was left to its successor bodies to give detailed information on the coefficients used;
- was based on a model that enabled identification of the earning power of individual departments or cost centres;
- funded teaching according to student numbers;
- was selective in research funding; and
- based research funding on quality assessments that might vary on a three- or four-year basis.

As a consequence, by the mid-1980s institutions were faced with:

- the need to address implied criticism from the Jarratt Committee on the efficiency and effectiveness of their management practices;
- the need to adapt their internal procedures to the new methodology for allocating institutional grants; and
- a continuing decline in the unit of resource from government with a consequential need to increase funding from non-government sources.

Critical issues ∎

These last three issues lead to a range of questions that continue to be critical to any discussion of the process of managing financial resources. These questions have been reached through a brief historical survey of the UK higher education system leading to the reforms in the mid-1980s, but the questions themselves have international applicability. As other writers have commented: 'no country today could provide through the state budget as much education as wanted by its citizens' (Psacharopoulos 1990). As a consequence, 'pressure to reform the financing of higher education has mounted in virtually every part of the world' (Ziderman and Albrecht 1995). This reform of higher education financial systems has increasingly led governments to establish funding councils or to review the basis on which the ministry of education funds higher education institutions.

Alongside these changes in governmental approach lie expectations that institutions will adopt increasingly efficient and effective internal mechanisms for the allocation and use of their resources. There are, therefore, two factors:

1 an inability of government to provide sufficient funding; and
2 the need for efficient and effective use of those funds that are available.

Whilst institutional leaders continue to lobby for an increased share of the national budget, it is the second factor that can be more immediately influenced by the action of institutional managers. Internationally, this action is being seen to embrace two trends:

1 A greater degree of devolution either from institutional to faculty, school or departmental level or from government to institutions as in former communist countries. As London (1996) has observed, the strategy of decentralization has been proposed in both developed and developing nations because it is believed 'to reduce abstraction in decision-making; to permit more prompt response to educational problems, and to clarify lines of accountability'.
2 The adoption of formulaic models in place of historically based allocations and the striking of annual bargains.

In the face of these international trends, what are some of the critical questions facing higher education institutions in relation to the management of financial resources? These may perhaps be categorized as relating primarily to funding models, devolution and other associated issues, although in practice there will be overlap between the categories. Some of these questions should be addressed as part of the normal decision-making process; others may well force themselves on the institution as consequences of reactive behaviour patterns.

Funding models

- To what extent should a national funding methodology be replicated at an institutional level?
- For what purposes should an institutional model be used? In particular to what extent will it inform managerial decisions or be a determinant of allocations?
- How will greater transparency in the national system and the increasing use of performance indicators affect behaviour patterns within the institution?

Devolution

- To what extent should responsibility for financial management be devolved to a cost centre level?
- Should a cost centre be at the level of a department, school, faculty or other grouping?
- To what extent should the administration be devolved?

Other associated issues

- Are devolved, formula-based systems of resource allocation seen as tools for allocating resources or as opportunities to change the culture of an institution?
- What will be the impact of new methods of resource allocation on the relationship between the academic community and senior administrators?
- How will the model be used in the wider managerial and strategic planning processes?
- How will the introduction of a model affect decision making?
- How will the effectiveness of the organization be evaluated?
- How can the danger of goal displacement be avoided?

The issues inherent in these questions recur in the following chapters, but in order to place in context later discussion a few preliminary observations are made at this stage. These are categorized under the headings of institutional culture, organizational structure, relationship between the academic community and senior administrators, concepts of power, impact of technology, and planning and evaluation.

A word of warning

Before proceeding, however, there should be a word of warning. As we observed in Chapter 1, organizations display a range of different characteristics (Handy 1993). Consequently, no single system or approach will be universally appropriate. This is as true within the UK system as it is internationally.

Within the UK

Institutional responses to changing patterns of finance in higher education were reviewed by Williams (1992). He noted that the development of systems based on financial devolution to departmental cost centres had become 'the post-Jarratt and post-corporate status orthodoxy'. More detailed studies of individual institutions during the late 1980s and early 1990s also drew attention to the acceptance of devolved, formula-based systems of resource allocation as conforming to the prescriptions of the times (Bowman 1990; Barnes 1991; Thomas 1997). Such approaches assume that the dominant loyalty of academics is to their subject-based discipline (Becher 1989), but, as Williams observed, a minority of institutions adopted an alternative approach of encouraging corporate loyalty to the institution as a whole. Of the institutions reviewed, four had substantial devolution to a departmental level and one to a faculty level; three devolved expenditure other than academic salaries to a departmental level; four reported partial devolution; and three claimed little movement towards devolution (Williams 1992: 29). Consequently, Williams saw models as 'points on a spectrum. At one extreme all resources – staff, space and consumables – are allocated centrally. At the other, faculties, schools or departments are autonomous budget centres meeting their own requirements for staff, space, consumables and administrative services from income that they themselves generate and control' (ibid.: 25).

In his study, Williams also isolated (p. 29) a variety of different meanings of devolution with big differences between institutions in:

- the formulae or other procedures by which departmental allocations are determined;

- the budget heads over which the department has control;
- the extent of virement between budget heads; and
- the possibility of carrying forward surpluses or deficits.

In conclusion, Williams recognized that, 'a variety of internal management structures have proved to be viable in coping with turbulent financial circumstances. The essential consideration is for institutions to have mechanisms for establishing realistic priorities, implementing strategic plans and ensuring that resources are not used inefficiently or wastefully' (ibid.: 38). Such an approach is consistent with that identified by Sharpe (1994) who, in a study of the Australian school system, sees responses to devolution in terms of a continuum.

What emerges, therefore, is that whilst devolved, formula-based systems of resource allocation grew in popularity during the 1980s and in some respects developed the standing of orthodoxy, the approach was not universally adopted. Nevertheless, institutions have continued to display a fascinating interest in the subject. Writing in 1998, 13 years after the Jarratt Report had set some institutions on the road to devolution, Webber (1998) was able to commence an article in *perspectives: Policy and Practice in Higher Education* with the observation that 'Devolved budgeting has become the new orthodoxy of higher education management' and two years later Weiler (2000) observed that European higher education had 'discovered a new game' incorporating performance-based models of resource allocation.

Internationally

The trends of devolution and formula-based systems have spread not only within countries of the British Commonwealth, where the structure and practices of higher education find their roots in the British system (Koder and Hewitt 1992; Sharpe 1994), but also in the USA, where there is interest in 'performance budgeting' (Schmidtlein 1999), in western Europe (Weiler 2000), and in the emerging democracies of central and eastern Europe and parts of Asia. In these emerging democracies, the development of such systems is being encouraged by funding agencies such as the European Union, Asian Development Bank and World Bank which see these management techniques as providing a foundation for the more efficient and effective use of resources. That may well be the case, but it often involves a range of associated issues such as the training of staff, use of technology, and implementation of appropriate structures, in addition to changes in culture and established practices, all of which take time to develop (Hall and Thomas 1999). Moreover, there is growing experience that warns against the dangers of transporting systems from one country to another (Tomusk 1995, 1997; Burton 1997; Billing and Thomas 2000). In central Europe, for instance, there is a tradition of direct funding of faculties by government. Rather than enhanced devolution, the issue here involves exploring ways in which the central university authorities can gain increased control in the interests of more effective planning for the institution as a whole (Thomas 1998; Littlewood 1999; Devinsky 2000).

What emerges, therefore, are no easy or consistent answers but a range of questions and issues that have to be addressed within the behavioural, cultural, technological and socio-economic environments in which individual institutions and systems have to operate. It is not the intention here to delve deeply into the theoretical context of these issues, but a little reflection might help to highlight and to set in context some of the more practical issues.

Institutional culture

Five main organizational models of the higher education institution might be identified:

1 *Bureaucratic* (Weber 1947), in which rules and procedures dominate and decisions are taken according to an established hierarchy of authority. It has been questioned, however, whether this state of affairs realistically represents the relationships that exist within an academic institution or whether in fact it is desirable within an academic context. As Moodie and Eustace (1974: 21) observed, what exists is 'an untidy diffusion of responsibility and a proliferation of centres of initiative and decision-making which are related to one another in ways which are not neatly bureaucratic. There is no direct and comprehensive chain of command, and the notion of an order being issued from one person to another is generally felt to be alien to the way in which British universities should govern their affairs.' This led to the concept of 'loose coupling' (Weick 1976).
2 *Collegial* (Millett 1962), which substitutes the concept of hierarchical decision making with the concept of community and consensus. It may be that many would regard the culture of collegiality as typifying the traditional university approach, but in reality it is likely to overstate the degree of consensus and shared authority that is normally obtained (see also Tapper and Palfreyman 1998, 2000).
3 *Political* (Baldridge 1971), which contrasts sharply with that of bureaucracy. Whereas the emphasis of the latter is on the system,

the political model stresses the role of the individual member of that system. In this model, the organization is seen as 'the convergent locus of the interests of multiple stakeholders' (Dore 1992: 17). Ideally, the relationship between personal and organizational goals would be where individuals perceive the organization as an avenue for professional growth (Thompson 1965; Nadler *et al.* 1992). Nevertheless, as Simon (1964) has pointed out, although personal satisfaction may arise from the competent performance of a professional role, the desire for power and concern for personal advancement represent an intrusion of personal goals upon organizational goals.

4 *Organized anarchy* (Cohen and March 1974), which modifies views of collegiality and includes concepts of power and preferences within a complex organization. Features have been seen to include: ill-defined goals; no obvious connection between the way work is done and the outcome; sub-units only loosely connected with the result that influences from external factors are contained within a small number of sub-units because of their autonomy; widely differing criteria of success operating simultaneously in various parts of the organization (Cameron 1980). The organized anarchy model may be particularly relevant to those institutions where the culture is strongly departmental and where devolution of budgetary responsibility is to the level of the basic organizational unit, defined as 'the smallest viable grouping in any academic institution, working within its own budget and, to a sizeable extent, its own terms of reference' (Becher and Kogan 1992: 102).

5 *Entrepreneurial* (Davies 1987; Clark 1998) in which there is created 'the ability to manoeuvre within fairly short time-scales to respond to opportunities' (Davies 1985: 54). The entrepreneurial university will be distinguished by the characteristics of an explicit, understood and visible mission; a focused and relevant portfolio of activities; a differentiated organizational structure with conventional departments and faculties alongside specialized units for the purpose of achieving multidisciplinary activities; and the emergence of powerful directors of key activities (Davies 1987). The model was developed in the 1980s in response to rapid changes in the external environment which made past practice less reliable as a guide to decision making. A significant consequence of these changes was the need for institutions to develop a positive attitude towards the need to extend their range of income streams. The model has more affinity with political models and the behaviour associated with them than with bureaucratic or collegial models, but Clark (1998) sees scope for collegiality to find space within the entrepreneurial university.

The definitions below are, of course, 'pure types' and in practice more than one cultural model is likely to be in evidence in any given institution, but shifts in the balance between models is likely to occur as the institution responds to external pressures. Building upon the work of Weick (1976), McNay (1995a) has suggested a four-phase cultural model using the concepts of collegium, bureaucracy, corporation and enterprise. The four quadrants (Figure 3.1) reflect the extent of looseness in policy definition and in control of implementation of policy. McNay implies that a clockwise movement is normal, with institutions moving from quadrant A through B and C towards D. Many of the post-1992 universities in the UK appear to be in the 'corporation' quadrant, reflecting the executive authority of the vice-chancellor and a small directorate. In terms of the management of financial resources, the model reflects well the tension within institutions. On the one hand, the need to make savings implies the culture of corporation; on the other hand, the necessity to seek new sources of income implies the culture of enterprise. It is for each institution to find its own balance between these competing imperatives. (See also Dopson and McNay, chapter 3 in Warner and Palfreyman 1996.)

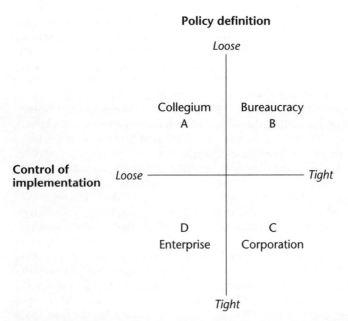

Figure 3.1 Models of universities as organizations

Organizational structure ▪

Extent of devolution

The extent to which institutions are centralized will need to reflect the relationship between strategy and structure. Galbraith identified three types of organization: functional, divisional and holding company, and three types of control: operational, strategic and financial. He suggests that, 'the degree of centralisation varies from high to low when we move from the functional model to the model of the holding company' (Galbraith 1993: 17). The level of control is summarized in Table 3.1.

Table 3.1   Degree of central control

Type of control	Type of organization		
	Functional	Divisional	Holding company
Operational	Central	Delegated	Delegated
Strategic	Central	Central	Delegated
Financial	Central	Central	Central

In the context of an institution of higher education, the degree of central control may be influenced by size, diversity, relative coherence of departments and the number of campuses. A specialist, single-faculty institution is likely to display functional characteristics; an institution with a wider range of disciplines may display characteristics of a divisional organization; whilst a large, multi-campus institution may display features of a holding company. In the context of the management of financial resources, however, it is significant that, whilst operational and strategic control may be delegated, ultimate financial control rests with the central authorities.

Level to which to devolve

In those institutions that intend to adopt devolved structures, there arises the issue of the level to which to devolve. The choice may be between devolution from the centre to departments or from the centre to faculties/schools, leaving the faculties/schools to determine the degree of further devolution to its departments. Becher and Kogan, in identifying the various levels as the individual, the basic unit, the institution and the central authority, suggest that 'the faculty level functions either as a molecular basic unit or as subsidiary to the institutional level according to context' (1992: 8). This context is likely to be influenced by the size of the institution and the historic bases of power. In institutions in which heads of department have traditionally wielded power, with deans acting as *primus inter pares* any attempt to create the faculty/school as the primary unit of resource management is likely to be seen as a challenge to the existing order. Of course, such a challenge may be intended, but senior managers will need to be prepared to meet the inevitable response.

Extent to which the administration should be devolved

If devolution is to take place to a department, faculty or school then an associated issue is the extent to which the supporting administrative structure should be devolved. The issue has been summarized by Balderston (1974: 79–80) as follows:

> If administrative functions are heavily centralized, they may operate in a tidy, professional manner, but without sufficient understanding of the administrative problems and needs of individual academic units. If these functions are decentralized, they may not be staffed by sufficiently qualified professionals and may develop inconsistent procedures and techniques. If the institution builds up administrative capability in these areas both at a central point and in the operating academic units, the total cost is enormous. Avoiding the worst of all three evils requires careful managerial design and effective administrative coordination.

The danger, as Beer (1972) has pointed out, is that if 'centralization' and 'decentralization' are treated as alternatives then the structure of an organization can alternate between the two depending upon fashion and the success of the enterprise at any given time. Much will depend upon the size and location of the academic unit, for physical decentralization may not be cost effective if devolution is to be to a departmental level. What is important, however, is that administrative personnel should 'become part of integrative problem-solving groups rather than resentful onlookers sharpshooting from the outside' (Thompson 1965). Consequently, there will be a need for what might be described as 'psychological devolution', with support staff seeing their role as facilitator and encourager and as an integral part of budget centres' hopes and aspirations whilst at the same time maintaining a monitoring role.

Relationship between the academic community and senior administrators

Under historical systems of funding, senior managers tend to have a monopoly on critical information. When a department's allocation is plus or minus a few percentage points on the previous year's figure, the baseline for that calculation is often lost in the mists of time or exists in the memory of the chief executive and a few senior officials. These factors place senior managers in a pivotal position to correlate and coordinate information from a variety of internal and external sources. They act at the interface between the external and internal environment. As such, they are the interpreters of the external environment for academic departments.

As institutions responded to a changing national funding methodology by moving towards a more numerate, analytical and systematic base for decision making, a number of changes have been noticeable. First, since the external methodology changed towards a more quantitative approach, it became more difficult to base an internal resource allocation system on previous historical factors. On the other hand, those historical factors had, hopefully, taken account of local priorities and preferences and been based on a decision-making mechanism that reflected the nature of the institution. There was, therefore, a tension between looking afresh at internal methodologies and accepting previous decisions based on subjective judgement of the prevailing internal situation.

Second, there was a shift of political influence into the hands of the officials who were most intimately involved in preparing the statistical base. The location of such persons in the institutional hierarchy may vary. They may be academic managers or professional administrators located in the registry, planning or finance offices. A critical criterion is not necessarily a financial background, but an ease with figures, a facility to use spreadsheets and an ability to explain the figures to non-numerate colleagues, particularly in academic departments. As systems of devolved resource allocation develop, staff at a departmental level require management information which they can readily understand. This requirement raises the profile of those staff in the central administration who have a responsibility for providing the information.

Third, whilst the 'numerate generalist' within the central administration gains in profile, there is also a sense in which power shifts away from the central administration and becomes more diffuse. Information disclosure is an essential element in increasing the level of participation of staff in decision making. The disclosure by the funding council of the details of the way in which institutional grants are calculated makes information available not just to those with inside knowledge of the funding council's workings, but to anyone who studies the various circulars issued by the funding council. To represent adequately their constituents, deans and heads of department need to understand the basis on which the institution's grant is calculated and the specific components that affect the financial position of their own faculty or department. This has the potential to affect the balance of power within institutions. No longer can senior officials hide behind some opaque funding methodology. The way in which the institution's grant is calculated is now open for all to see. This alters the balance between academic departments and the central administration and also the balance between academic departments. Academic reputation as an internal pecking order gives way to a differentiation between those departments in surplus and those in deficit.

Concepts of power ■

Although many issues of financial management may appear technical in nature, to a considerable degree they are influenced by the exercise of power, whether the basis of that power be bureaucratic, professional, coercive or personal (Baldridge 1971). Consequently, any significant change in methodology is likely to affect the balance of power. As Stacey (1993: 190) has observed: 'Any sign of change will touch off fears that such power shifts might occur even before it is clear what they might be. People and groups will therefore start taking protective action as soon as they get wind of any possible change.'

This concept of power is particularly appropriate in the context of the resource allocation process. It has been seen during the discussion of the Jarratt Report that the recommended changes in management practices were aimed at curbing the influence of powerful individuals. However, there is evidence to suggest that the implementation of supposedly more rational systems of resource allocation does not reduce what Hoyle (1982) has described as the 'micropolitics of organizations' but merely shifts its focus away from the annual budget exercise to the process by which the details of the internal allocation model are determined (Thomas 2000). Whilst senior managers may be under pressure to improve resource allocation mechanisms, for most members of staff the critical issue, as it has always been, is not how budgets will be allocated but 'who shall receive budgetary benefits and how much' (Wildavsky 1961).

For those who are interested in pursuing the matter further there is a range of interesting material on the relationship between power and the resource allocation process. A number of factors emerge from the literature:

- Although the language of resource allocation 'is cloaked in the appearance of objectivity and neutrality, it is ultimately directed towards establishing and maintaining hierarchies of authority and status' (Covaleski and Dirsmith 1988).
- Sub-unit power is an important determinant of budget allocations within organizations (Pfeffer and Salancik 1974).
- Sub-unit power accrues to those departments that are most instrumental in bringing in or providing resources which are highly valued by the total organization, for example grants and contracts and student enrolment (Salancik and Pfeffer 1974; Pfeffer and Moore 1980).
- In turn, this power enables these sub-units to obtain more of those scarce and critical resources allocated within the organization (Salancik and Pfeffer 1974).
- Whilst, in times of abundance, allocation is according to accepted standards (workload) and a fair-share criterion, during periods of scarcity of resources, powerful sub-units 'emerge to claim their resources at the expense of other subunits' (Hills and Mahoney 1978).
- Core units (i.e. those that are central to the mission of the institution) 'benefit when they help themselves', whilst peripheral units gain 'when they contribute to the total institution' (Hackman 1985).

Impact of technology

The introduction of devolved formula-based resource allocation models can require the provision of a level of management information which has not previously been made available. Consequently, the limitations of existing systems and associated technology can be exposed. As Fielden (1993: para. 3) has said: 'information flows are crucial; . . . they affect the viability of the whole system, since inadequate, untimely or inaccurate information can destroy the basic purpose of delegating decisions'.

Decision making has been classified into the areas of strategic planning, management control, and operational control (Anthony 1965). As Ewart (1985) has recognized, although the information needs at each of these different levels are different, there is a degree of dependence and overlap between one category and another. Moreover, this three-part classification describes not only the institution as a whole but also each of the relatively autonomous units within it. Consequently, there is a range of information needs which, whilst appearing different in detail, need to be comparable and should be part of one overall system. There is a danger that devolution without an adequate information system will force budget centre managers to create their own local systems. Lack of integration can then lead to misunderstandings as to the underlying financial position of the institution. Ewart highlights five important characteristics of a technology-based information system:

1 integral part of the organization's ongoing activities;
2 man–machine system involving the integration of manual and computer systems;
3 collection of sub-systems, some of which may be closely linked, others loosely coupled;
4 technology based to make the best opportunities of current and future potential; and
5 belongs to the institution as a whole not the technology experts.

These characteristics will play a significant part in determining whether an institution is prepared for the introduction of a devolved, formula-based system of resource allocation. (See also Elkin and Law 2000.)

Planning and evaluation

Expansion of the higher education system, external pressure for more effective management and a decline in financial resources have had an impact on institutional planning and evaluative mechanisms. In particular, the following trends are noticeable:

• Institutional planning has gained a higher profile and mission statements have increasingly provided evidence of the goals of the institution. These goals, however, are the official goals of the institution. They give no hint of the numerous decisions that must be taken to differentiate between alternative ways of achieving the stated goal or between the priority of multiple goals. Nor do they differentiate between the many unofficial goals pursued by groups within the organization. As implied in the above section on power, there can exist a tension between the official goals of the mission statement and the operative goals that 'tell us what the organization actually is trying to do, regardless of what the official goals say are the aims' (Perrow 1961: 855). Such an approach explains how different organizations with the same official goals might use different means towards achieving their ends. In terms of recent trends in financial management, care needs to be taken to ensure that the additional workload involved in creating a resource allocation model does not focus excessively on operative goals to the detriment of official goals, otherwise resources might be diverted away from academic endeavour to the extent that 'the administrative cost of the system could offset the gains from better housekeeping' (Shattock and Rigby 1983: 66). As Gaskell (1989) has observed, there is a danger that demands are placed on academic staff which are at odds with scholarship. In these circumstances goal displacement becomes an issue.

- The use of performance indicators has become more widespread as an evaluative tool. In terms of financial management the relationship between performance in attracting income and internal allocations has become greater. As Cameron (1980) points out: 'no single approach to the evaluation of effectiveness is appropriate in all circumstances or for all organizational types', but as higher education has expanded it has become noticeable that 'the link between the allocation of resources and evaluation became stronger and more explicit' (Becher and Kogan 1992: 157). Consequently, the use of formulaic models indicating the surplus or deficit of each cost centre has become an important evaluative tool. In an academic institution, however, such approaches are measures of 'operative' effectiveness and need to be set against evaluation of the 'official' academic goals. These comments imply a relationship between evaluation and institutional goals, but an alternative approach is to view evaluation from the perspective of sub-units, each balancing its own situation with that of other sub-units in a social justice approach emphasizing personal satisfaction or equity regarding organizational activities (Keeley 1978). Thus heads of department, for instance, will harness quantitative evaluation with their own subjective and political arguments to portray their departments in the best possible light. Consequently, 'evaluation cannot be separated from the constant interplay of values, judgements, conflicts, motives and emotions of people. In this sense it operates within a highly charged political arena' (Batten and Trafford 1985: 297).

An holistic approach

The above sections have been directed towards an explanation of some of the underlying issues affecting the management of financial resources. It will have become evident that the process is multifaceted and will be approached in different ways by different institutions. Nevertheless, many of these factors are interrelated. Consequently, in working through the following chapters a constant theme will be needed to maintain equilibrium between a range of institutional variables, shown in Figure 3.2 as task, technology, structure and people.

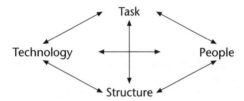

Figure 3.2   The Leavitt diamond

Consistent with this model, the process of financial management affects:

- tasks expected of members of staff including income generating activities, the monitoring of performance, the adoption of effective procedures and practices and a general emphasis on managerial functions;
- technology used in the process to ensure integration of data that is timely, consistent and easily understood by a wide range of users;
- structure of the institution in terms of establishing planning and resources committees, mechanisms for resource allocation and the appropriate level to which devolution should take place; and
- people and their expectations, training and development needs, staff appointments and promotion criteria and behaviour patterns.

None of these variables is static, however, so that 'change in any one usually results in compensatory (or retaliatory) change in others' (Leavitt 1965: 1145). Failure to appreciate the interrelated nature of these variables may lead to a period of mismatch (Donaldson 1987). Moreover, changes to these variables can be consciously intended, or they can occur as unforeseen and often costly outcomes of efforts to change only one or two of the variables (Leavitt 1965: 1145). As Kochan and Useem (1992: 404) have said: 'The technological, organizational, and human resources must be altered together, since the potential of one can be fully realized only when developed with all.' Moreover, given the necessity for institutions to engage in income-generating activities to compensate for declining government funds, resource allocation mechanisms may be seen as being as much about cultural change as the technicalities of financial management. In these circumstances, 'organizational change is not just a matter of changing technologies, structures, and tasks. More fundamentally, it entails a change in values and beliefs that employees hold' (Mohrman and Lawler 1993).

Consequently, when addressing issues of managing financial resources in the following chapters a constant theme will be the need for an holistic approach to ensure that 'dynamic equilibrium' is maintained between these institutional variables (Scott Morton 1992) and that institutions can respond quickly and effectively to external pressures (Shattock 2000). In this context a balance needs to be found between what Stacey (1993) has termed the 'extraordinary management' of innovative organizations (represented here by the need to encourage flexibility, responsiveness and income-generating activity) and the 'ordinary management' of bureaucratic systems (represented here by the need to ensure sound financial practices).

A three-stage approach

The above sections have delved lightly into some of the theoretical frameworks that underpin issues associated with the management of financial resources. The next three chapters are concerned with more practical issues. The basis of these chapters is that any process of resource allocation requires an understanding of income streams, application of strategic considerations and allocation of resources to activities or constituent parts of the institution. A subsequent chapter will focus on the process of monitoring. It is, therefore, suggested that the resource allocation process should consist of three stages (Thomas 1999) as outlined diagrammatically in Figure 3.3.

• *Stage 1* will involve determining how the funding council's formula affects the institution. This is essential information required by senior managers and should reflect, through raw data, the funding council's model at an institutional level as an aid to managerial judgement. It will also involve data showing other sources of income. Anything beyond this first stage of management information

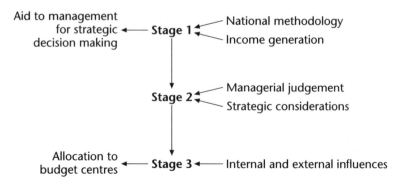

Figure 3.3 Stages in the resource allocation process

 begins to involve internal decisions which will be influenced by institutional and personal preferences and priorities and which will be determined by both rational and micropolitical factors.

* *Stage 2* will involve the application of strategic considerations and managerial judgement to these raw data. Both stage 1 and stage 2 provide valuable management information to senior staff. By incorporating data on expenditure they provide a profit and loss account for each budget centre. As a method of evaluation, it should be expected that the figures will be used not only at an institutional level as a basis for strategic decision making, but also by heads of department as part of the micropolitical debate.

* *Stage 3* will involve the institution in deciding upon its method of allocating resources to budget centres. Recent external pressures have increased the likelihood that stage 3 will be based, at least in part, on a formulaic approach, but the extent to which this is so will be conditioned by a range of factors that are explored in a later chapter.

Each of these stages forms the focus of one of the next three chapters.

4

THE ALLOCATION PROCESS 1: UNDERSTANDING THE INCOME

Introduction

The previous chapter outlined three phases in the resource allocation process: understanding sources of income, application of institutional strategic considerations, and distribution to the various faculties, schools, departments or activities within the institution. This chapter is concerned with the first of these phases. It falls into the following parts.

Funding council income

This section will review the annual funding cycle and the methodology adopted for the allocation of grant to institutions, focusing in particular on the teaching and research components. The thrust of the chapter is on the issues raised by funding methodologies, leading to consideration of the way in which changes in external methodology impact on internal procedures. Such considerations are likely to be as relevant in countries where there is direct funding to institutions from the ministry of education as in countries with a quasi-independent funding body. Since methodologies for funding institutions in the UK have changed over the years, and no doubt will do so again, any discussion of detailed methodology can only be for the purposes of illustration. England, Scotland, Wales and Northern Ireland have their own funding arrangements. Examples in this chapter are drawn from the Higher Education

Funding Council for England (HEFCE), the largest of the funding agencies.

Other income

As was mentioned in Chapter 1, it is only in the past 50 years or so that the state has assumed responsibility for the vast majority of expenditure on higher education. The shift in emphasis towards a reduction in government expenditure per student highlighted by the government cuts of 1981 and continued in the form of 'efficiency gains' in succeeding years may, therefore, be seen in historical terms as a reversal of a temporary period of substantial government subsidy. There are, however, substantial differences between the pre-war and post-1981 periods in the size of the higher education system and the diversity of the student population. For most institutions, there now exists the need to compensate for a declining unit of resource with an increase in income from non-government sources through entrepreneurial modes of activity.

There was a time when non-government income was referred to as 'soft money', reflecting the fact that such funds were additional to the necessary running costs of the institution. As government funding has declined, this 'soft money' has become indispensable to cover shortfalls between income from government sources and the cost of providing an adequate learning and research environment. As a consequence, and as McNay (1995b) has noted, some institutions now regard their governmental income as soft, being subject to the vagaries of government policy. In this part of the chapter we will review the major sources of income other than from the funding council and will reflect upon the shift towards students paying for an increasing proportion of their costs in undertaking higher education.

Issues

Arising from the review of the various sources of funding, a range of issues will be identified and discussed in such a way as to lead to the content of the next two chapters which are concerned with institutional responses. The issues to emerge will be influenced by such factors as the balance between institutional autonomy and public accountability, concepts of efficiency and effectiveness, commercialization of activities, the changing market and cultural change. These are wide issues, but the discussion will be restricted to those aspects of the subject that impinge on the management of financial resources.

Funding council income ■

Annual funding cycle

Institutions of higher education receive notification of their grant from their funding council in March for the following academic year. This is the culmination of a process begun twelve months earlier. The various stages in that process, as it applies to institutions in England, may be summarized as follows (HEFCE 1999):

- *April–November*: the funding council advises the Department for Education and Employment (DfEE) on the trends and financial needs of higher education for the next academic year.
- *November*: the secretary of state for education and employment announces the level of funding to be made available for higher education and informs the funding council of the total grant to be made available to it. This is accompanied by advice on spending priorities. The total grant is agreed each year by parliament.
- *December*: higher education institutions and further education colleges provide the funding council with information on the distribution of the current year's student numbers. The main return from higher education institutions is known as the Higher Education Students Early Statistics Survey (HESES). A similar return is provided by further education colleges. This return is known as the Higher Education in Further Education: Students Survey (HEIFES). Further education colleges are involved in this process as they receive funding from the HEFC for their higher education students. They receive separate funding from the Further Education Funding Council in respect of students registered for further education programmes. It is on the basis of these returns that the following year's grant for teaching is calculated. Thus the student numbers in year Y go towards the calculation of grant for year Y + 1. During the same period, higher education institutions provide information on research activities. This information goes towards the calculation of the following year's grant for research.
- *January*: the funding council decides the distribution of the total grant between the main headings, namely teaching, research and other funding. Most of these funds are distributed by formulae, taking into account the volume and mix of individual institutions' teaching and research. The data on which calculations are based are published so that institutions can check the outcomes. The publication of this level of detail is one of the significant changes in practice in recent years. The proportions between

Table 4.1 Distribution of total funding, 1999/2000

	£m	%
Teaching	2916	69.2
Research	855	20.3
Special funding	435	10.3
Flexible margin	10	0.2
Total	**4216**	

teaching, research and other funding are roughly the same from year to year. In 1999/2000, total funding amounted to £4.22 billion distributed as shown in Table 4.1.

This grant was allocated to 402 institutions in England made up of: 71 universities, 16 colleges of the University of London, 47 higher education colleges, and higher education courses in 268 further education colleges.

This allocation was based on 921,700 full-time equivalent students for 1998/99 distributed as follows:

– Undergraduate: full-time   74 per cent
                             part-time   15 per cent
– Postgraduate: full-time   5 per cent
                             part-time   6 per cent

• *February*: the funding council decides the distribution of grant to universities and colleges.
• *March*: the funding council announces the distribution of grant to universities and colleges.

Funding methodology

In the years since 1986 when the UGC announced its new funding methodology breaking from historical practices, the methodology adopted by the funding council has undergone a number of revisions. In particular, the replacement of the UGC by the UFC in 1989 saw a move towards greater disclosure of the details of the funding council's model. The unification of the university and polytechnic sectors as a consequence of the Further and Higher Education Act 1992 required the newly established funding councils to devise a methodology suitable for the enlarged sector of higher education. In 1998/99, the HEFCE changed its method of allocating funds for teaching on the basis that, whilst the previous method provided stability for institutions, in some cases it maintained historical levels of funding that were inequitable. This desire to break away from historical inequities had found expression in the UGC's motivation for change in 1986. Currently, there are suggestions that the funding methodology does not adequately reflect or encourage the diversity of activity and institutional mission found within the expanded higher education system (Brown 2000). It cannot be assumed, therefore, that the latest changes to the funding council's methodology will be the last. The implication for institutions is that their internal funding methodologies have to be sufficiently robust to withstand changes in external funding regimes.

It is not the purpose here to describe in detail the current funding methodology. The latest details can be found in documents published by the funding councils. There are, however, certain principles underpinning the methodology for funding teaching and research which have remained fairly constant over the past ten years or so. These are as follows.

Support for teaching and learning

The calculation is made up of two elements:

- The number of students in each institution as returned each year by the institutions (see above). These numbers form the basis of the financial calculations for the following year's grant.
- The price associated with the teaching and learning process. Some subjects are more expensive to teach than others. Accordingly, the funding council funds different categories of student at different levels. The present methodology adopted by the HEFCE is to divide students into four broad price groups. The price for a full-time equivalent student covers grants from the funding council and tuition fees. Those four groups together with the cost weight and price for 1999/2000 are:

– Clinical subjects	£12,060 (cost weight 4.5)
– Science, engineering and technology	£5360 (cost weight 2)
– Other high-cost subjects with a studio, laboratory or fieldwork element	£4020 (cost weight 1.5)
– All other subjects	£2680 (cost weight 1)

These standard prices are subject to some variation to take account of certain additional costs affecting specific types of student or specialist colleges.

Research funding

Funding for research comes from a variety of government and non-government sources. Government funding is channelled through both the funding councils and the research councils. We consider the latter under the section below on other income; we are here concerned with that portion that is allocated by the funding councils. This is intended to cover the basic structure needed for research, including the salaries of permanent academic staff and the cost of premises and central computing. Unlike the teaching component of the grant, the funding councils allocate research funds selectively so that universities and colleges with high quality research departments receive a larger share of the money. There are two components to the calculation: quality and quantity of research.

Quality of research is assessed through a periodic research assessment exercise (RAE). The first such exercise was conducted in 1986, with subsequent exercises in 1989, 1992 and 1996. As with the teaching methodology, the details of the RAE have varied over time, but in essence they are as follows:

- Institutions are invited to submit for assessment within a number of subject areas (currently 69). The number within which any institution will submit will depend upon the range of academic disciplines covered by the institution.
- Evidence submitted will include research outputs mainly in the form of publications in academic journals, but may include any other form of academic research, for instance, artistic performances.
- These submissions are assessed through a process of peer review, with panels of experts being formed for each subject area.
- Each submission is given a quality rating judged against standards of national and international excellence. When the exercise was commenced in 1986 there were four categories: excellent, above average, average and below average. In 1989, a numeric scale was introduced ranging from 1 to 5. This was continued for the 1992 exercise, but for the 1996 exercise it was thought necessary to subdivide points 3 and 5. Thus a seven-point scale emerged: 1, 2, 3b, 3a, 4, 5, 5*. Each of these ratings represents a level of national or international standing as follows:

5* Research quality that equates to attainable levels of international excellence in a majority of sub-areas of activity and attainable levels of national excellence in all others.

5   Research quality that equates to attainable levels of international excellence in some sub-areas of activity and attainable levels of national excellence in virtually all others.

4   Research quality that equates to attainable levels of national excellence in virtually all sub-areas of activity, possibly showing some evidence of international excellence, or to international level in some and at least national level in a majority.

3a Research quality that equates to attainable levels of national excellence in a substantial majority of sub-areas of activity, or to international level in some and to national level in others comprising a majority.

3b Research quality that equates to attainable levels of national excellence in the majority of sub-areas of activity.

2   Research quality that equates to attainable levels of national excellence in up to half the sub-areas of activity.

1   Research quality that equates to attainable levels of national excellence in none, or virtually none, of the sub-areas of activity.

For the purposes of managing financial resources, the critical issue is the way in which these judgements of quality are converted into institutional grants. To do this, the funding council converts the quality scale into a funding scale. The conversion table for 1996 is shown in Table 4.2.

Table 4.2   Quality rating to funding weight conversion table, 1996

Research quality rating	Funding weights
5*	4.05
5	3.375
4	2.25
3a	1.5
3b	1
2	0
1	0

Thus, a department rated as 1 or 2 attracted no research funding. A 5* department attracted a little over four times as much money as a department rated as 3b. Over successive research assessment exercises the element of selectivity has been increasing. In the 1986 exercise, all departments, even those rated as below average, received something. In the 1992 exercise, it was only grade 1 departments that did not receive anything. We discuss some of the consequences for institutions of this policy of increasing selectivity in a later chapter. For the present it is sufficient to note two factors:

1 that institutions have sought to increase their research grading; and
2 that the amount of money available for distribution according to
research criteria has not kept pace with the increase in grades.

A consequence of these two factors is that from one RAE to the next,
departments have had to improve their grading simply to receive the
same funding.

Quantity of research is determined according to factors such as the
number of academic staff actively engaged in research, the number
of postgraduate research students and the research income from
charities. This again has changed over time. For instance, student
numbers rather than staff numbers were used in the first RAE. A
significant factor under the current system is that institutions themselves decide how many academic staff are deemed to be research
active. This is important because funding is determined by multiply-
ing the quality rating by the quantity of activity. For those institutions in which the research quality of staff is variable, it is a matter
of judgement as to whether they submit a large number of staff and
risk a lower quality rating or try to achieve a high quality grade
by restricting the number of staff they submit. This was a particular issue during the 1992 exercise, which was the first to include
institutions in the former PCFC sector. As a consequence of the
1992 experience, many institutions formed the view that there were
advantages in seeking a high quality rating and became selective in
the staff they submitted for the 1996 exercise. It should be noted,
however, that figures published by the funding councils show not
only the RAE quality rating but also the percentage of staff submitted. Unfortunately it could be argued, insufficient attention is
given to this column of information. It cannot be assumed, for
instance, that all staff in a grade 5 department are producing research
at attainable levels of national or international excellence. It is only
those staff who have been submitted who have been so judged. This
reflects a tension as to whether the research assessment exercise is
primarily a funding mechanism or an assessment of quality. For
potential research students, the attraction of being accepted by a
highly rated research department may seem obvious, but further
enquiry needs to be made to ensure that the potential supervisor
was included in the list of staff contributing to the assessment.

Special funding

In addition to the teaching and research elements in the grant allocation, the funding councils also allocate funds for special initiatives.
These are aimed at supporting innovative projects and for infrastructural

improvements. Examples of such funding include projects to develop good practice in teaching and learning, grants for research equipment, support for students with disabilities, grants for continuing education courses and UK-wide projects such as the network linking universities and colleges. The method of allocating funds for special initiatives involves a process of competitive bids from institutions. Proposals are then assessed against set criteria.

Other income ■

Government sources

Government grants represent about 40 per cent of institutional funding, although this percentage will vary between institutions. There are, however, other sources of government funding.

Tuition fees paid by local education authorities

In addition to grants from the funding council, teaching is funded through tuition fees. For most students on full-time undergraduate courses these were paid by local education authorities. In 1996/97, this source of income accounted for about 12 per cent of institutional funding. For 1998/99, many new UK and EU undergraduate students on full-time higher education courses had to make a contribution towards the cost of their tuition. The fee level was set at £1000 per year, which represented about a quarter of the average cost of tuition. This increased to £1025 for the following year. Fees are means-tested so that students from poorer families are exempt or pay only a proportion.

Research council grants

Whilst the funding councils provide the basic structure for research through the research component of their grants (see above), the research councils provide for direct project costs plus a fixed percentage to cover indirect costs. The research councils also support some postgraduate students. About 5 per cent of institutional income comes from the research councils.

Non-government sources

In addition to government funding, institutions are free to raise income from other sources without its affecting their government grant. The main sources of income, which have grown in importance as government funding per student has declined, include the following.

Overseas student fees (about 5 per cent)

When the government withdrew its subsidy to overseas students in 1979 there was concern that the number of overseas students would decline, with an adverse effect on long-term international relations. There was indeed a reduction in numbers for a short period, but in the longer term there has been an increase in the number of overseas students in UK higher education institutions. This is partly a reflection of the standing in the world of UK higher education, but it also reflects the marketing efforts which institutions have put into this area of activity (Humfrey 1999). In fact, competition from the USA and Australia, for instance, to attract good students is intense.

Efforts to establish good relationships with institutions, particularly those in the Far East, have been seen to pay dividends in providing a stream of 'full-cost' students. In more recent years this market has been extended through the establishment of franchise arrangements under which it is possible for students at an overseas institution to study for an award from a UK institution. The motivation for such activity has been primarily financial, but equally important in such partnerships is the establishment and maintenance of quality assurance procedures. The extent to which institutions have pursued the overseas market has differed, and as a consequence the percentage of an institution's income that is dependent upon the maintenance of overseas student numbers is variable. There is a danger that such a market could be volatile. It is, therefore, a matter of institutional judgement as to the extent to which income from this source should be used to underpin long-term activities.

Other fee income (about 8 per cent)

In the past this has included primarily fees paid by postgraduate students, part-time undergraduate students and students on short courses. In the future, if full-time undergraduate students are required to make an increasing financial contribution to their tuition, this category of income will increase in percentage terms.

Other income from research and services rendered (about 15 per cent)

In addition to support from the research councils, institutions may undertake contract research for industry (about 7 per cent) and for

UK charities (about 3 per cent). There is also a range of other non-research services which institutions provide (about 5 per cent).

Residences and catering (about 7 per cent)

This is an area that has been a focus of attention by institutional managers in their efforts to raise non-government funds. Whereas there was a time when the residences and catering operation was seen as geared in essence to students' needs, the approach has become far more commercial. Student residences, for instance, are now built to a standard that will satisfy the demands of the conference trade. It is also not unusual for student accommodation to be let during vacations as holiday accommodation.

Endowments (about 2 per cent)

Although for most institutions the income from endowments will be small, this is another area that has been seen as having potential for growth. As a consequence, there has been increased attention paid to alumni relations in the hope that maintaining contact with former students may bring financial benefits in the long term.

Other operating income (about 7 per cent)

This will include interest on deposit accounts and returns from stock market investments. It is not always appreciated that one of the roles of the finance office is to ensure a good return on both long-term *and* short-term investments ('treasury management').

Issues

The previous paragraphs have outlined the various sources of funds available to institutions of higher education. Understanding these sources is the first stage in the process of managing financial resources. This involves, however, not merely an appreciation of the range of available sources but also an appreciation of issues and implications for institutional management. This section discusses some of those issues and implications under three main headings: the effect of the current funding methodology with its character-istics of transparency, selectivity and formulaic basis, the need for institutions to raise non-government funds, and the need to adopt a client-orientated approach.

Current funding methodology

The development of the RAE raised a number of important issues for institutions:

- Changes in research assessment on a three- or four-yearly cycle, feeding as they did into financial allocations, created a volatility in funding that had to be addressed within internal funding models.
- The RAE was both an assessment of quality and a funding mechanism with both qualitative (the RAE rating) and quantitative (staff numbers) coefficients. Institutions became wise to the tactical possibilities of influencing their rating through careful choice of which members of staff to submit. For some the choice was between high volume/lower average quality and low volume/higher average quality.
- At a departmental level there were implications for the distribution of duties amongst academic staff. The funding implications of the RAE forced departmental managers to focus staff on activities where they could be most effective in financial terms.
- RAE judgements were based on certain recognizable criteria. This encouraged institutions to focus on activities that would gain RAE 'brownie points'. There was a danger that such a reaction would be inconsistent with the creation of a diversified higher education system.

The need for institutions to raise non-government funds

It has been seen in earlier chapters that the changing environmental context has led to cultural change within institutions and to the development of entrepreneurial activity. The following are some of the practical manifestations of this changing environment:

- The need to recognize the increasingly competitive nature of the environment.
- The need for internal resource allocation methodologies to include incentives for departments to raise income.
- The need to recognize in promotion and salary discussions the value of staff who are successful in attracting outside income.
- The danger that pressurizing staff to raise income may divert them from an academic focus.
- The danger of seeking external funds for their own sake without any added value to the academic enterprise.

- The need to ensure that external projects and activities attract sufficient overhead income to ensure that costs in terms of staff time and the use of facilities, equipment and consumables do not outweigh the income from the activity.
- An implication that heads of department and deans need to assume a greater financial management role as well as their traditional role of academic leadership.
- An implication that criteria for appointment of professors and senior staff may well need to include managerial expertise as well as academic credentials.
- The need for development and training programmes in financial management for staff who have risen to managerial positions through an academic or non-financial background.
- A reorientation on the part of staff in the central administration and particularly in finance offices to provide a facilitative function to support staff in academic departments who are undertaking managerial and income-generating activities.
- The need to ensure that mechanisms are in place to provide consistency of data between records maintained in departments and those maintained by the central administration.
- A need to ensure that data provided by the central administration are in a form that is easily understood by those not familiar with accounting conventions.
- The need to ensure within academic departments an equitable distribution of work amongst teaching, research, income generation and other activities. Many departments, for instance, operate a 'brownie points' system to ensure comparability of workload between staff.
- The need to recognize that quality in terms of research output not only attracts income from the funding councils through the research component of the annual grant, but can contribute to income generation through reputation, to the marketing of programmes and to the gaining of research grants and contracts.
- The necessity to recognize that, whilst income generation through research activity has a direct impact on income, teaching activities attract income through student numbers and indirectly through reputation.
- The necessity to enhance investment income.
- The necessity to focus on alumni activities.
- The necessity to appoint staff with a commercial or marketing orientation. Catering and sports facilities, for instance, and indeed space in general, all need to be managed to generate income that can be used to support the academic enterprise.
- A change in the nature of staff appointments in the central administration. The dominance of the generalist has given way to

appointment of an increasing number of specialists who might bring with them skills acquired outside the higher education arena.

The need for institutions to adopt a client-orientated approach

The move from an elite towards a mass system of higher education has changed the profile of the student body, with an increase in the numbers of mature and part-time students. This has been accompanied by government policies that have required an increasing contribution from full-time undergraduate students towards the cost of their education. Although their impact on the management of financial resources may not be as immediately apparent as other policy changes, these factors raise a number of issues of growing significance, including the following:

• The relationship between student and staff has changed. In particular, students demand value for money. As a consequence, a client-orientated approach is necessary if students are to be recruited and maintained.
• There is a need to provide counselling services to advise students on financial issues. Some institutions have established services to help students find part-time employment during the term to help them fund their studies.
• Libraries and computer services have increasingly extended their opening hours to meet the convenience of a wider range of students.
• Crèche and nursery facilities have been established to cater for the children of students.
• Staff have increasingly had to make allowance for the non-academic concerns of students. A wider profile of student has brought a wider range of problems, but if student numbers are to be maintained, with the associated funding, more flexible approaches have to be taken when dealing with student issues.
• A flexible approach has also had to be taken to the payment of student fees. If students are themselves paying a proportion of their fees, some may be unable to pay as a lump sum in advance. Consequently, payment by instalments has become more widely accepted, providing an added procedural and monitoring burden on the staff of finance offices.
• Procedures are necessary to deal with any cases of genuine hardship in meeting payment terms. This will involve the administration of a hardship fund.

Conclusion ■

In this chapter we have reviewed income streams, an understanding of which forms an essential first stage in the management of financial resources. In the light of recent trends, issues were identified which have implications for institutional managers. In the next chapter, attention turns from these external factors to some of the internal strategic issues that are likely to influence the way in which the income is distributed amongst the various component parts of an institution.

5

THE ALLOCATION PROCESS 2: STRATEGIC AND INSTITUTIONAL CONSIDERATIONS

Introduction

The focus of the previous chapter was on understanding the sources of institutional income, whether that income came from government sources or through income-generating activity. In particular, the funding council's calculations of the teaching and research components of annual institutional grants were considered. This process of understanding income streams represented the first stage in a three-stage model of resource allocation. In practical terms, this stage provides institutional managers with a model showing the pattern of income distribution amongst different departments, faculties and schools of the institution.

In this chapter we move to stage 2 of the process. This involves the application of strategic considerations and managerial judgement to the raw data emanating from stage 1. The development of formulaic approaches by the funding councils, combined with a need to encourage income generation, has created pressure on institutional managers to create models for internal resource allocation that reflect the way in which the institution receives its income. We shall consider in Chapter 6 the distribution process (stage 3), but it is the contention of this chapter that it is unwise to jump from stage 1 to stage 3 without an intervening stage in which strategic considerations and managerial judgement are applied.

This second stage is consistent with the funding council's declared policy. Although the calculation of institutional grants is made up of a number of component parts, taking account of teaching and research factors across a range of departments, the funding council has continued to stress that what emerges from the process is a block-grant. This block-grant can be distributed within institutions at the institution's own discretion provided that it is used to support teaching, research and related activities. Institutions are accountable to their funding council, and ultimately to parliament, for the way in which they use council funds. As we have seen, they are also free to raise money from other sources. This allows them to provide additional support for teaching and research and to pursue activities alongside those for which they receive council funding. There is, however, significant pressure on institutions to provide financial monitoring information at a cost centre level. Cross-subsidies between cost centres and between teaching and research activities, therefore, need to be justified on strategic grounds. Interestingly, despite long-standing references to the block-grant principle by the funding councils, the possibility of more directed allocations in the future cannot be ignored. We return to this topic in Chapter 7, on monitoring, but it underlines the thrust of the current chapter that resource allocations need to be based on sound strategic considerations.

Constraints on institutional managers

Whilst the principle of the block-grant supports the concept of institutional autonomy, in practice the increased transparency and the formulaic approach adopted by the funding councils since the mid-1980s has introduced some practical constraints on institutional managers. These constraints have come in two forms: technical and behavioural.

Technical constraints

Technical constraints have been seen in particular in relation to student numbers. When government wished to see an increase in student numbers, institutions were encouraged to recruit 'fees-only' students. However, when government policy changed to one of consolidation rather than expansion, the concept of maximum aggregate student numbers (MASNs) was introduced to ensure that institutions recruited within designated targets. Significant under- or over-recruitment could make the institution liable for a financial penalty.

Behavioural constraints

Whilst technical constraints may be seen as externally generated, behavioural constraints will be governed by internal factors associated with the micropolitics of the organization. At a time when the UGC's funding methodology was clouded in mystery, heads of department and deans were reliant on historical precedent and the power of their personality and departmental standing to influence the resource allocation decisions of senior managers: just the sort of influence that the Jarratt Committee attacked. Once the funding council's methodology became more transparent, there appeared an additional tool in their armoury: the figures published by the funding councils themselves. No longer were deans and heads of department reliant on the interpretation of senior managers, they now had the same figures on which to base their calculations and arguments.

This meant that the behaviour patterns of senior managers themselves had to change. No longer was historical precedent a sufficiently rational explanation for resource allocation decisions. If the funding council could break from historical allocations in the calculation of their grant to institutions, then there was no reason why central administrators could not break with historical precedent in the allocations to faculties, schools and departments.

It was, however, not only the comparative allocation amongst academic units that was called into question. There was also the issue of the division of funds between academic and administrative departments. Since the funding council allocates funds according to teaching and research criteria, a model showing how income is attracted to the institution will distribute funds amongst academic units. To finance administrative sections, these academic units will need to be 'taxed'. This concept then opens the way to debate about what administrative services are required, the most cost effective way of providing those services, and who has authority over how those administrative services are conducted. There is likely, for instance, to be debate about:

- the extent to which administrative services should be devolved to a faculty, school or departmental level;
- the extent to which academic departments are required to use the central services, for instance, whether the institution's printing unit should have a monopoly on institutional business or whether academic departments should have the freedom to use commercial companies;
- the way in which the costs of the library and computer centre are divided amongst user departments;

- whether departments should be charged for space to cover such expenditure as heating, lighting and maintenance; and
- the range of expenditure to fall on the budgets of academic departments as opposed to the central administration.

Planning cycle

The above are some of the issues that are likely to be raised as part of the debate about the resource allocation process. In essence, however, they are details that condition the nature of the resource allocation methodology. Each institution will find its own answer to these issues. Within the framework that is established, however, there will need to be consistency and a degree of rationality in the resource allocation process if the institution is to achieve its strategic objectives. For this reason, financial management should be seen as part of an annual planning cycle that consists of agreement on strategic objectives, the allocation of resources consistent with those objectives, agreement of budgets within the resources allocated, monitoring of financial performance against the budget, application of performance indicators to monitor progress towards achievement of strategic objectives and a review of strategic objectives (Figure 5.1).

This annual cycle shown in the figure is a generalization of the routine adopted in many institutions, but it highlights two particular points of interest: the order of the resource allocation and budgetary processes, and the link between performance indicators and resource allocation, indicated by the broken line.

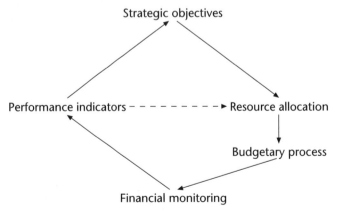

Figure 5.1   Annual planning cycle

Order of the resource allocation and budgetary processes

The question is sometimes raised about the order of activities, in particular whether the budgetary process should precede the allocation of resources. This issue has tended to change over time and may still vary between institutions or between different sectors of the institution.

In the days before the adoption of transparency and formula-based approaches by the funding council, it was often the case that internal institutional allocations were determined ostensibly on the basis of budgetary submissions made by each academic and administrative unit. Considerable effort was made by heads of department to formulate an annual budgetary submission which showed the need for increased expenditure. These submissions were considered by a central university committee, which then allocated funds which, in many cases, did not differ greatly from the previous year's allocation. In this cycle, the budgetary process would have preceded the allocation process. With the advent of allocations from the funding council that can clearly be identified in terms of academic units, the tendency has been to allocate funds to departments and to require departments to produce a budget based on the allocation.

This begs a question, however, and that is the way of determining the division of funds between the central administration and the academic departments. It is not unusual for this initial division of funds to be based on need, determined by budgetary submissions from non-academic units. In effect, there is often a top-slicing process to determine non-academic allocations. There is a danger that this may put non-academic units at an advantage. The institution, therefore, needs to take care that if, in any given year, there is any difference in percentage increase or decrease between academic and non-academic areas then the rationale for such a difference is clearly specified and explained. Ideally the allocation process to non-academic areas will have involved academic members of staff to ensure ownership of the process and decisions by the institution as a whole. In reality, the relative treatment of the academic and non-academic areas is likely to be fraught with micropolitical activity and to be a source of potential mistrust and mutual suspicion.

Link between performance indicators and resource allocation

The process of institutional monitoring has increasingly seen the adoption of performance indicators of a financial nature. With a transparent methodology being adopted by the funding council and pressure to encourage staff to seek non-government sources of income, a particular performance indicator has become the financial health of each basic unit in the institution. This in turn has created pressure to ensure that those departments that attract funding for the institution should themselves directly benefit from their efforts. Consequently, as Becher and Kogan (1992) have observed, there has become pressure for a closer relationship between indicators of income-generating performance (whether that income comes from the funding council or other sources) and resource allocation.

Clearly, for the sake of maintaining incentives for income generation, there has to be some correlation between income generation and income distribution, but the process needs to be set within the context of the strategic objectives of the institution. As the broken line on Figure 5.1 shows, if there is a direct relationship between income generation as a performance indicator and the resource allocation process, the strategic planning aspect of institutional management may be omitted to the detriment of the institution as a whole.

Strategic planning

This is not the place to expound at length on the planning process. Those who wish to pursue the topic might consult a chapter on strategic planning in Warner and Palfreyman (1996), or Watson (2000); and there is much that is still of relevance in an earlier book by Lockwood and Davies entitled *Universities: The Management Challenge* (1985). In this last volume, Lockwood defines planning as 'the continuous and collective exercise of foresight in the integrated process of taking informed decisions affecting the future' (p. 167). The thrust of this present chapter is that the management of financial resources has to be seen as part of this integrated process. Two models are used to exemplify the point, the first relating to horizontal integration (academic, financial, personnel and space considerations), and the second to vertical integration (strategic, tactical and operational considerations).

Horizontal integration

This model (see Figure 5.2) brings together many of the behavioural and technical issues featured in Chapter 3, and incorporates:

Internal

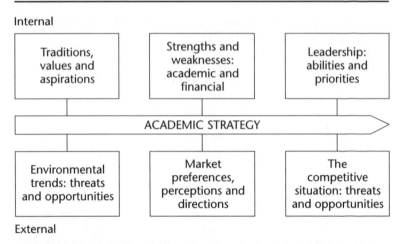

External

Figure 5.2 Factors influencing a planning strategy
Source: from Keller (1982)

- the internal and external pressures influencing the planning process;
- the influence of institutional culture and history;
- the strengths and weaknesses of the institution;
- the priorities and preferences of key personnel;
- both micropolitical and more rational aspects of decision making;
- subjective and objective criteria of decision making;
- the opportunities and threats offered by the prevailing environment;
- the agreed mission of the institution and the way in which it perceives itself in the higher education market;
- the competitive situation in relation to other institutions; and
- opportunities for collaboration.

All these factors will influence both academic and business activities of the institution, incorporating staff, space and financial considerations. To quote Lockwood (1985: 169): 'in terms of horizontal integration, the teaching, research, financial, personnel, social and physical aspects should not be seen as separable branches of planning which can be conducted in isolation'. This view was underlined by the Jarratt Report (1985) which referred to the need to establish strategic plans 'which bring planning, resource allocation and accountability together into one corporate process linking academic, financial and physical aspects' (para. 5.5a). In case there should be any remaining doubt about the practical importance of integrating financial management within a realistic planning process that takes account of both internal priorities and external pressures, it is worth remembering that there have been some high profile cases of institutions that have encountered financial difficulties. In reviewing three such cases, Shattock (1992: 249) stated that: 'all three institutions seem to have based their policies on a false view of the external environment'.

These factors are given graphic dimension in Figure 5.2, a model adapted from Keller (1982) which highlights six principal planning strategy elements.

Examination of this model provides a clear indication of why resource allocation, as part of the wider planning process, is concerned with far more than models and formulae and will involve subjective judgement as well as objective criteria. No two institutions are identical. Each has its own traditions, values and aspirations; each will have its own strengths and weaknesses; and the abilities and priorities of the leadership will vary. Consequently, the move towards formulaic approaches to resource allocation at a national level provides a new challenge for institutional managers. Some of the immediate questions that arise include:

- How are the individual characteristics of institutions to be maintained in the face of pressures towards common funding mechanisms?
- How are weaknesses to be addressed when it is the strong departments that attract funding?
- How can institutional priorities shift the status quo when funding is based on current activities and past performance?

Strategic planning should be focused on decision making. That involves not only an assessment of current strengths and weaknesses, but also an assessment of the external environment and a view of how this will affect the future of the institution. To avoid simply reacting to events and trends, the strategic planning process should position the institution to take advantage of anticipated changes in the environment and itself to influence those changes to its advantage. In terms of financial management, that may mean the redirecting of resources, pump-priming new initiatives to be prepared for change, or restructuring current activities to better meet customer demands. In terms of Keller's model, this is reflected in the need to assess external threats and opportunities and to assess market preferences, perceptions and directions.

The extent to which institutions will be able to respond to this external environment will depend upon their ability to use funds flexibly. Again, however, the external funding methodology may provide support for conservative forces within the institution, for change may imply shifting financial support away from areas that currently attract income towards new areas where income streams are not yet established. The ability to make such change will depend upon a number of factors, including:

• The financial health of individual academic units. It is easier and more acceptable to expand a new area by reducing surpluses in other areas than by increasing deficits.
• The culture of the institution. Palfreyman (1989) has written about how the University of Warwick faced the challenges of the 1980s by pulling together as a cohesive unit to make a reality of the concept of an entrepreneurial university (see also Clark 1998). Other institutions, however, may be more departmentally based, with power residing with heads of department who see their first priority as protecting the interests of their discipline and department. In institutions in which this departmental culture is prevalent, the gaining of consensus and the employment of flexibility in the use of funds are likely to be more difficult than in institutions in which there is a collegial ethos.
• The extent of non-government income. Declining government funds force institutions to adopt more entrepreneurial approaches. Not all institutions, however, have the facility to earn large amounts of non-government income. Perhaps most opportunities arise in the institutions with large science and engineering departments. The ability to use resources flexibly, including the top-slicing of funds for new initiatives, will be that much easier within an institution with the ability to generate income. Even in such institutions, however, senior managers are likely to have to deal with internal pressures from heads of income-generating departments who will press strongly for income earned to be allocated to the income-generating department rather than being designated for activities elsewhere. A balance will need to be drawn between the maintenance of incentives by rewarding income-generating departments and the creation of new opportunities by top-slicing income from departments in surplus.

Vertical integration

The above model of horizontal integration focused on the importance of locating financial management within the wider process of institutional planning. That process itself has a vertical dimension (Figure 5.3) incorporating:

• strategic planning with a timescale of perhaps three to five years;
• tactical planning on an annual basis; and
• operational planning being the daily decision-making process.

O
R
G
A
N
I
Z
A
T
I
O
N

Strategic planning: 3–5 years

Tactical planning: annually

Operational planning: daily

Figure 5.3   Vertical integration
Source: from Simon 1961

Integration between these three levels of the planning process is critical to the achievement of an institution's objectives. In terms of financial management, there is a need for:

- financial data to inform strategic planning decisions;
- annual allocation of funds to be consistent with the achievement of the strategic plan; and
- daily decisions to support the institution's priorities.

In this regard, the adoption of an internal resource allocation model that is widely understood and is accepted by the institution as a whole can help to bring an element of consistency between the different levels of the planning process. The value of such a model at each of these three levels is explained below.

Strategic planning

At the level of strategic planning, an income and expenditure model can provide a valuable analytical tool serving as a basis for the various decisions that need to be taken in order to move the institution forwards. It is at this level that the senior management team will be operating and will need to be able to assess the impact of a range of alternative decisions on the financial health of the institution. A model that is capable of manipulation to respond to 'what if' questions is essential in the management of an institution in today's complex environment. Given the use of spreadsheets it should be a relatively simple process to project for a number of years the effect of an increase or decline in overall budgetary levels on any given cost centre as well as on the institution as a whole. Similarly, it is possible to see the long-term financial effect of, for instance, a change in student or staff numbers or a shift in resources between different sectors of the institution.

Consultation, communication and debate within the institution as a whole should be a priority at this level. The drafting of documentation and the creation of planning and financial models are likely to be in the hands of a small group of central managers, but successful implementation is likely only if there is wide discussion and ownership within the institution. This debate is likely to engender a wide range of views, many based on self-interest or the interest of that section of the institution being represented by participants. Such micropolitical activity should be accepted as part of the planning and resource allocation process. As Bruton (1987) has observed: 'the production of an academic plan and allocations to cost centres is unlikely to be reached with full agreement by all parties. Rather it will more than likely be adopted after prolonged bargaining sessions amongst the leading protagonists, and arbitration through majority decisions of Senate and Council.' In times of financial restraint, this political element in the decision-making process has been seen to grow in importance.

Tactical planning

Historically, one of the problems in institutional management has been to ensure consistency between the strategic objectives of an institution and the annual allocation of funds to achieve those objectives. There is always the danger that external pressures and short-term internal crises can blow an institution off course and divert it from achieving its goals. The existence of a financial model which informs the decision-making process at all levels of an institution can provide a focus during the annual allocation process with a view to the making of decisions that are consistent with strategic objectives.

It is also at this level that a financial model, consistently operated with clearly defined coefficients, can give to heads of department a framework in which they can calculate their annual budgets and undertake their own long-term planning. For example, if it is known that a certain percentage of the fees from overseas students will be allocated to the department teaching those students, heads of department can calculate the effect of an increase in the number of such students. Similarly, if there is virement between salary and non-salary expenditure heads, a head of department can calculate the effect of staff vacancies and consider how best to use any savings accruing to the department. As mentioned elsewhere, however, the use of a model in this way can have the adverse effect of polarizing debate between departments in surplus and those in deficit.

Operational planning

The utilization of an income and expenditure model can help to focus individual members of staff on the importance of their contribution to the welfare of their department. When successful student recruitment, research grant applications and recognition through the RAE are seen to have a direct effect on departmental income, the incentive for effective personal performance becomes clear. Of course, a system that makes individuals aware of their contribution to the income of their department also brings consequential demands for an allocation of funds to those responsible for the income generation. These demands may be related to personal salaries or promotion opportunities. They may also be related to research and teaching support, for instance additional equipment and facilities or time to focus on certain activities. This may be achieved through study leave or a reduction in workload in other areas of the department's activities. Conversely, such a model can focus attention on staff who are a financial drain on a department and can raise critical issues for heads of department to address in their planning strategy. More is said about managing financial resources at a departmental level in Chapter 8. For the present, however, it is sufficient to note that the external environment has led to an increase in the management of academic activities at a departmental level, with added demands on heads of department.

Reflections

The above sections have located the management of financial resources as an integral part of a wider planning process in which the necessity for horizontal and vertical integration have been emphasized. It was seen that the development of an income and expenditure model can contribute to the achievement of integration between the strategic, tactical and operational layers of the planning process. However, experience in the use of such models leads to some practical observations:

- At a strategic level, a formula-based model showing the financial health of each basic unit can provide consistency between the strategic direction of the institution and budgetary allocations.

However, the development of such models may imply a radical redistribution of resources compared with the historical pattern. Attempts to rectify such anomalies might be neither desirable nor possible in the short term because of high fixed costs. Consequently, judgement will have to be applied to mitigate over-dramatic effects.

- The use of such models, together with other performance indicators, provides valuable quantitative data to aid the management process. However, the management process remains complex in nature, involving both quantitative and qualitative information and both rational and micropolitical elements. Consequently, formulaic approaches do not absolve senior managers from the responsibility of applying subjective judgement in the decision-making process.
- Such models clearly highlight those departments in surplus and those in deficit. There is a balance to be achieved between meeting the ambitions and demands of departments in surplus which will wish to expand and develop their activities, and supporting financially weaker departments that are making a valuable academic contribution to the institution as a whole.
- Such models are sometimes developed in response to external pressures. Consequently, there is a degree to which they are used not only for internal management purposes but also to provide evidence that an institution is conforming to perceived managerial norms.
- Such models clearly display a department's income streams and by implication identify income-generating capacity of individual members of staff. Inevitably, therefore, such approaches influence managerial actions and priorities at a departmental level and impact on the status and activities of individual members of staff.
- There is a general implication that managers at all levels have to be capable of interpreting quantitative data. They have to be numerate, analytical, politically aware and conscious that the existence of such models may not in fact ease the decision-making process.
- Such models can polarize opinion between surplus and deficit departments.
- Within a turbulent external environment, a formula-based resource allocation scheme can offer a degree of consistency and certainty with predetermined incentive schemes which are welcomed by departments as a positive element in their financial and academic planning. However, if such a model has to be suspended or abandoned these positive features are lost with a consequential negative effect on staff morale.
- As is implied in the three-stage model advocated in Chapter 3, such models may be used for evaluative purposes or as a basis for the allocation of resources. The link between evaluation and the allocation of resources may be exacerbated by the development of

formulaic approaches as there is pressure on institutional managers to reflect directly the evaluation criteria (namely the income achieved) in the level of allocation.
- The use of such models increasingly leads institutions to evaluate their basic units on their ability to attract resources. The inherent danger of such an approach is that it submerges academic quality beneath a financial evaluative tool.

These general observations may be supplemented by a range of more specific practical issues that managers are likely to face during this second phase of our three-phase approach. These might include, for instance, the following:

- What percentage of its 'earned income' should be allocated to a cost centre? For instance, should the whole of the fee from overseas students be allocated to departments teaching the student? Should the recruiting department be allocated an extra share of the income to reflect its efforts in recruitment? Should there be a 'top-slice' from the fee income to reflect demands on central services?
- If a department is in deficit, is it intended that the department should become financially viable? If so, what is a realistic timescale for that expectation to materialize? What steps will be put in place to ensure the timescale is kept?
- On what basis will surplus departments be 'taxed' to compensate for deficit departments?
- How will new initiatives be funded? Will there be a central pool created from a 'tax' on departments? How will that fund be allocated? Will there be a bidding process? It was seen in Chapter 4 that the funding council allocates a small proportion of its funds on the basis of competitive bids. Should the institution adopt a similar procedure?
- How will oscillation in funding be approached? For instance, the RAE might lead to periodic changes in income. Over what timescale will departments have to adjust to their new level of funding? To what extent should such income be used to fund long-term commitments?

These issues will be approached by institutions in their own way. It is worth reiterating that, whilst the external environment and the funding councils' methodology for calculating institutional grants have placed pressures on institutional managers to act in certain ways, there is no one uniform method for distributing resources within an institution. In the next chapter we consider in more detail some of the influencing factors.

Conclusion

In this chapter we have been concerned with bridging the gap between understanding the way in which income is attracted to the institution and the way in which it is allocated to the various activities or constituent parts of the institution. A number of essential points arose from the analysis:

- Resource allocation and financial management in general are part of an annual cycle in which strategic planning forms an essential component.
- For institutions to have control over their own futures the resource allocation procedures must incorporate flexibility.
- Flexibility depends upon acceptance that income cannot be allocated directly according to a model of how that income is earned.
- Changes in resource allocation methodology are as much about cultural change as about methods of financial management.
- The internal allocation process is likely to incorporate micropolitical as well as rational elements.
- Ownership of the process will best be achieved if institutional leaders can engender a sense of collegiality amongst the component parts of the institution.
- There needs to be confidence in the methodology adopted for allocating funds to the central administration.
- Cognizance needs to be taken of the rate of change that it is possible to achieve.
- Local culture and traditions will shape the strategic choices of individual institutions.
- The personalities involved will influence the decision-making process.
- Communication and consultation throughout the institution are essential if there is to be confidence in the resource allocation and financial management processes.

The thrust of the chapter has been that it is the responsibility of senior managers to locate the financial management process and in particular the allocation of resources within the process of institutional planning. The chapter has advised caution in allocating funds according to the way in which they are earned. That is not to say, however, that there should not be an internal resource allocation model, but rather that this model should reflect internal priorities and preferences rather than simply ape the model of an external agency.

If we bear in mind the annual cycle shown in Figure 5.1, the successful implementation of an institution's strategy is likely to be dependent upon an allocation and budgetary process that is consistent with the strategic objectives of the institution. That process will need to be monitored (see Chapter 7) and progress towards the achievement of strategic objectives regularly reviewed. Those strategic objectives will need to build upon internal strengths and aspirations and take cognizance of external opportunities and threats.

6

THE ALLOCATION PROCESS 3: DISTRIBUTION OF RESOURCES ■

Introduction ■

In this chapter we are concerned with the way in which financial resources are distributed within the institution, but before continuing, let us recap on the previous two chapters. In Chapter 4 we reviewed the way in which income was attracted to institutions and reflected on the consequences of the funding councils' adopting transparent funding methodologies that enabled identification of the extent to which each component part of the institution attracted income. In Chapter 5 it was argued that any model that was based on raw data from the funding councils would need to be subject to adaptation in the light of strategic considerations and managerial judgement before being used to inform the process of internal resource distribution. In this chapter we take the process one stage further by considering the various factors that influence the internal methodology to be adopted. This is the final stage of the three-stage model outlined in Chapter 3.

As Fielden (1982: 176) has observed, planning models may be categorized as ranging somewhere along two separate spectra: the dictatorial to the participative; the qualitative to the quantitative (Figure 6.1).

The quadrant in which any particular institution will be placed will be determined by its culture and the preferences and priorities of its senior managers. Indeed, the position of an institution may well change over time as influential staff change. The style of a new chief executive is likely to be particularly influential in the methodology adopted. Size and subject mix will also be determining factors. In large institutions, moreover, with a devolved management structure,

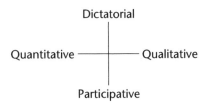

Figure 6.1   Classification of internal resource allocation systems
Source: Fielden (1982)

it is possible that different sectors of the institution will adopt different styles. The approach at a central institutional level might be quantitative and towards the dictatorial end of the spectrum, whilst a faculty may adopt a more participative and qualitative approach in allocating resources from the faculty to a departmental level. As we have observed in Chapter 3, however, whatever style and methodology are applied for allocating resources and whatever the institution's policy on the degree of devolution adopted, the ultimate responsibility for financial management lies with the institution centrally, and in particular with the chief executive and senior officers.

Recent trends indicate that there are two issues that have dominated managerial thinking:

1 the extent of devolution; and
2 the extent of adopting formulaic systems.

In addressing these issues we need to bear in mind that devolved, formula-based systems of resource allocation may be seen primarily in terms of the technical process of allocating resources or as an attempt to change the culture of an organization as a matter of policy. Such a policy may be aimed at challenging the established departmental hierarchy or bringing the reality of the external environment to a departmental level in order to enhance income through an entrepreneurial approach. Whatever the primary intention, however, the main protagonists of change will need to recognize that both the technical and cultural environments will be affected.

Trends towards enhanced devolution to a departmental, faculty or school level tend to be accompanied by methods of resource allocation that are based on a formulaic approach. This is because the logic of devolution implies that managers at the budget centre level need to know that certain actions will lead to certain consequences: for instance, that a decision to increase the number of overseas students or to put effort into running a short course or conference will lead to a known percentage of the income from that activity being credited to the cost centre, or that a decision not to fill a vacant post will result in savings to the cost centre rather than their being absorbed within a central institutional pool. Thus, from the viewpoint of both reflecting the external environment and creating incentives, devolution tends to be accompanied by formulaic approaches.

Concept of devolution

A critical issue facing institutions is the extent to which devolution will enhance the efficient and effective management of resources, particularly at a time of increasing environmental pressure when qualities of adaptability, flexibility, responsiveness, decisiveness and speed are at a premium (Nadler *et al.* 1992: 2). Findings from studies indicate that there are often two assumptions underlying concepts of devolution: first, that the concept is a natural response to a turbulent external environment, and second, that effective academic units will be effective managerial units. Both these assumptions, however, can imply a dangerous oversimplification of the situation facing institutional managers.

Devolution as a natural response

The first of these assumptions ignores the wide range of responses adopted by institutions. In reality, there will be a number of factors that influence the level and extent of devolution. Moreover, although the rhetoric may be in terms of devolution, managerial approaches and actions clearly demonstrate that the concept of devolution itself has different interpretations amongst institutions and even amongst individual members of staff within the same institution. To take examples from two institutions in which senior managers were advocating greater devolution:

- At the first institution, the concept of devolution implied a responsibility on heads of department for the management of a single-figure budget, incorporating salary, equipment and recurrent expenditure. Alongside such devolution came virement between budget heads and the ability to carry forward from one year to the next surpluses and deficits.
- At the second institution, devolution was envisaged as the allocation of resources through a formulaic approach, but without heads of department having responsibility for a single-figure budget. Virement between budget heads was limited and salaries were to remain a central charge.

In both cases, however, senior managers were speaking in terms of devolution to enhance the awareness of external pressures at a departmental level.

Effectiveness of academic units

The second assumption, that appropriate academic units necessarily form the most effective management units when devolved financial responsibility is to be increased, again ignores the complexity of the cultural and managerial environment and in particular the size and discipline of departments. In many institutions there has always been a limited degree of devolution to the level of the basic unit, usually a department. It is natural to assume, therefore, that any additional devolution will be to this same level. To be effective, however, a substantial degree of devolution requires an environment in which funds can be used flexibly. That may not always be consistent with devolution to a departmental level, the reasons for which will be explored below.

Implications

These considerations lead to the implication that enhanced devolution should not be regarded as an automatic response to a turbulent external environment. Whilst there is a strong view that, in today's competitive world, devolution should be regarded as a major managerial approach, providing the opportunity for greater flexibility and speed of response, this view needs to be sensitive to a multiplicity of factors. These factors may either restrict the degree of devolution that is appropriate or influence its nature or implementation.

Formula approach ◼

We turn now to the second of the major issues: the extent to which formulaic approaches are to be adopted in the allocation of resources. As argued in Chapter 3, the introduction of a new methodology in resource allocation at a national level has affected internal institutional mechanisms. In order to determine future strategy, senior managers need to know how the funding council's formula relates to the activities of their basic units and how that income, together with any additional earnings, compares with the expenditure being incurred by those units. These raw data should inform the planning process, but for reasons explained in Chapter 5, automatic determination of departmental allocations on the basis of a formula designed to calculate an institution's block-grant is unlikely to be in the best interests of the institution. Nevertheless, to a greater or lesser extent, institutions may use an internal formulaic model in the resource allocation process. Depending upon circumstances, this internal model may be used to determine allocations or it may be used to inform senior managers who will then apply subjective judgement.

The use of planning models in higher education had received increasing attention since the early 1970s (see, for instance, Bleau 1981; Shattock and Rigby 1983; Cave *et al.* 1988). Performance indicators have included, for instance:

- unit costs to compare the financial performance of similar departments;
- staff/student ratios in determining whether to fill vacant posts or to approve the establishment of additional posts;
- the weighting of postgraduate students in determining a department's student load to encourage the recruitment of such students; and
- an academic staff/secretarial staff ratio and an academic staff/technical staff ratio to determine the number of secretarial and technical posts appropriate to each department.

The characteristic of systems that use such performance indicators is that they tend to be centrally controlled. They do not provide the opportunity to use funds flexibly by being able to use savings in one area to supplement expenditure in another area. They also reflect the historical tendency to view planning primarily in academic terms rather than recognize that academic aspirations have to be consistent with financial, staffing, space and technological resources. The trend since the mid-1980s, therefore, encouraged by the Jarratt Report and the funding councils' methodology, has been to move towards holistic approaches that require budget centres to operate all their activities within a single-figure allocation.

There are therefore four key issues:

1 Whether to adopt a formula-based approach.
2 Whether that approach will be based on a single income and expenditure model or whether there will be a range of formulae for different components of the allocation.
3 The extent to which a model (if adopted) will be used as an aid to managerial judgement or as a determinant of allocations.
4 The extent to which the model will reflect the methodology of the funding council.

Determining factors ■

When addressing issues associated with the introduction of devolution and formula-based systems there is no single criterion to be applied. It is here suggested that the range of factors may be divided into two categories:

1 Those that influence the advisability of devolving substantial financial management responsibilities to a cost centre level (*prerequisites*). These will include suitable senior staff appointments, staff training, support mechanisms, adequate management information systems and effective monitoring procedures. Without the existence of these elements the successful implementation of enhanced devolution will be seriously impaired.

2 Those that influence the nature of the system to be adopted (*determinants*). These will include the history and culture of the institution, its size, subject mix and organizational structure, financial health of the institution and its component parts, activities of powerful interest groups, the preferences and priorities of key staff and strategic priorities.

These factors are discussed below. Some are equally applicable to devolution and formula-based systems. Others may be more applicable to either devolution or a formulaic approach. To avoid duplication they are considered together. A summary is given in Figure 6.2.

Prerequisites
- Suitable senior
  staff appointments
- Staff training and
  development
- Support mechanisms
- Adequate management
  information systems
- Effective monitoring
  procedures

Determinants
- Organizational structure
- Organizational culture
- Size
- Subject mix
- Financial health
- Priorities and preferences
  of key staff
- Activities of powerful
  interest groups

Devolved formula-based systems

Figure 6.2   Factors influencing devolved formula-based systems of resource allocation

Prerequisites

Suitable senior staff appointments

The introduction of devolved, formula-based systems of resource allocation has implications for the selection and appointment of senior staff, particularly at a departmental, faculty or school level. In some institutions, heads of department or deans may not be seen as powerful figures, maintaining the tradition of 'chairmen' rather than managerial 'heads'. In such circumstances, the background and inclinations of those appointed may not be consistent with the requirement to manage large-scale budgets. As a consequence, implementation of a system of enhanced devolution would require the central authorities to take a more proactive role in the appointment of staff at these levels. In these instances there is a tension between the pressures for enhanced management capability and the culture of the institution. There is here a further conflict between the managerial and academic imperatives, for judgement about the most suitable candidate to fill a senior academic post may be influenced by a candidate's managerial as opposed to academic credentials.

Staff training and development

Such changes imply a programme of training and development for academic and administrative staff as part of a wider organizational learning process. There is a danger that recognition of a training requirement follows the change process rather than being used to prepare staff in advance. Some of this training will be in-house to ensure that local procedures and practices are well understood and to give an opportunity for internal discussion. There are, however, benefits in arranging regional programmes where heads of department, for instance, can exchange experiences and discuss problems with colleagues from other institutions. Such programmes can give a wider perspective and an opportunity to exchange views and work through issues away from the immediate working environment.

Support mechanisms

Staff training and development will be insufficient without adequate institutional support for those holding managerial responsibilities. This support will require the provision of adequate management information systems, as will be discussed below, but it will also require the support of administrative personnel and the formation of management teams to ensure that academic managers are not swamped with detailed tasks that can be delegated. There will also be a need for support and good communication from committees and senior managers within the central administration to ensure consistency of strategic direction. All this implies that enhanced devolution can be costly and time consuming unless adequate preparation is made. Moreover, the required support mechanisms must include clear rules and procedures for budgetary control and the monitoring of expenditure, the features of which are explored further below and more specifically in Chapter 7.

Adequate management information systems

Enhanced levels of devolution, particularly when associated with a formula-driven system of resource allocation, require the provision of timely, consistent and easily understood information from a system that is designed to meet the needs of academic departments and the central administration and the various task areas of the institution. From a systems perspective, there is a danger that variations in the nature of budget centres might lead to the growth of different management information systems and that a multiplicity of budget centres will increase the difficulty of establishing a campus-wide integrated system. Failure to ensure that such a system is in place before the level of devolution is increased can lead to duplication of effort, an increase in overhead costs and a potential for serious financial mismanagement. Past history may, therefore, make it prudent to delay the introduction of a devolved, formula-based system until such issues have been addressed. It will also need to be appreciated that the development of such a system will require political as well as rational argument.

The coefficients in any formulaic model must be clear and widely accepted. Care should be taken to ensure that principles underlying the methodology are capable of being converted into practice. For instance, systems that base financial allocations on student load are dependent upon the accurate and timely calculation of annual student load figures. The ability to provide such data may be dependent upon the capacity of the management information system and the workload and priorities of staff.

Effective monitoring procedures

Essential to any system of financial management is the existence of effective monitoring procedures. The essence of devolution is empowerment to basic units to encourage a response to market forces, but this does not absolve the central administration from establishing adequate budgetary control mechanisms and the monitoring of performance. Clear rules and procedures must be established to cover such issues as virement and the carry forward of surpluses and deficits. These rules and procedures will need to be particularly stringent where devolution incorporates salary costs. In such cases there needs to be a balance between encouraging entrepreneurial activity at a budget centre level and ensuring effective central control, particularly over long-term commitments. Chapter 7 is devoted to issues of monitoring.

Determinants

Organizational structure

There is a range of issues that will influence the extent to which financial management is centralized or devolved. These will include:

- the extent to which the institution is based on a departmental, faculty or school structure;
- whether these units are primarily academic units with their heads acting as chairmen on a rotational basis or whether they are powerful managerial units;
- the relationship between these units and the central institutional authorities; for example, whether managerial authority lies at the centre or at a departmental level or at an intermediary level such as a faculty or school; and
- whether faculties and schools (where they exist) act as a basic unit or as an intermediary unit.

These issues are important in terms of the management of financial resources since there is evidence to suggest that if a budgetary unit is created which superimposes a level of management responsibility above that already existing, the new unit will need to create a secondary distribution to the level that is already in operation. This can lead to an increase in administrative tasks. Moreover, the establishment of new structures can lead to micropolitical activity focused around existing centres of power.

As a consequence, there are dangers in creating structural change when there is no historical or cultural base to support that change. It is possible, of course, that structural change may be introduced to inculcate cultural change. In such circumstances, however, senior managers need to recognize that successful implementation will be dependent on strong support from the central management team. A particular issue to be addressed will be the need to appoint heads of budget centres who are structurally and individually more powerful than the heads of the constituent parts of that budget centre and who have the capability to act in a managerial rather than a chairmanship role.

Organizational culture

The above organizational characteristics will be reflected in the prevailing institutional culture. If we refer to the discussion of culture in Chapter 3, an important consideration will be the quadrant of McNay's model in which the institution lies – collegium, bureaucracy, corporation or enterprise. Factors will include:

- the extent to which the institution is driven by senior managers;
- the extent of discretion allowed to deans and heads of department;
- whether the concept of enterprise has taken root;
- whether there is a feeling of collegiality within the institution or whether the primary sense of belonging is to a department; and
- the balance between reducing expenditure, which implies the tight central control of a corporation culture, and income generation, which implies the devolved characteristics inherent in an enterprise culture.

Once these issues have been recognized, the critical issue is whether the institution, or perhaps more accurately the senior managers, wish to build on the existing culture or whether they wish to use methods of managing financial resources to shift the culture of the institution. Cultural change requires a recognition that the institution is a collection of individuals and that staff have to be prepared for the change. Change to an entrepreneurial culture, for instance, requires not only consideration of issues of efficiency and effectiveness, but also a sensitivity to the people-orientated issues of skills, style and shared values. Such an approach is dependent on changing the attitude and value systems of individuals and on encouraging flexibility and informal networks. This applies both at a departmental level where increased devolution will bring an enhanced managerial role for heads of department and in the central administration where the emphasis of the work will shift towards a more interactive, interpersonal and facilitating function. This need reflects the fact that as institutions respond to diminishing resources by becoming more managed institutions, there is a danger that the tension will increase between the bureaucratic, executive elements and the collegial, professional elements.

Size

A key issue is the relationship between the size of budget centres and their ability to respond to financial pressure. This can affect the items that it is appropriate to devolve to them. If salary expenditure, for instance, is to be devolved, this is likely to represent a high percentage of a department's total expenditure. As a consequence, a large budgetary unit will be necessary to make the concept of flexibility a reality. A figure of fifty members of staff has been suggested as a minimum. For many small departments, particularly those in deficit, devolution of salary costs can raise levels of concern without creating the ability to improve radically their financial position because of the high percentage of fixed costs.

This may suggest that small departments should be amalgamated into a larger cost centre for budgetary purposes, but before any such decision is taken it is important that cultural considerations be considered. Such amalgamations are most likely to be successful in circumstances where there is a natural professional coherence between the basic units and a history of working together. Even in these cases, however, tensions might arise if heads of department have been accustomed to managing autonomous units.

Subject mix

There is some evidence that the ability and willingness of heads of department to manage the additional responsibilities engendered by increased devolution may differ between disciplines. Through their professional backgrounds and experience of handling large research contracts, science-orientated heads are often more adept at responding to the issues than their arts-based colleagues. This can affect not only internal management of departments, but also micropolitical activity, with science-based heads of department having a greater facility to interpret and manipulate the data during debate. Figure 6.3 portrays

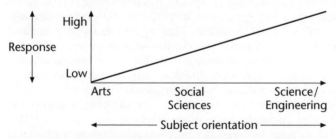

Figure 6.3 Responsiveness to devolution

the responsiveness to devolution that might be expected of the various departments in general.

Financial health of the institution and its component parts

A shift to a new system of resource allocation can shift the shape of the institution either as a matter of policy or as an unintended consequence. This might be particularly so in those cases in which the institution is moving from an historical allocation of resources to a system based on reflecting more accurately the way in which income is attracted to the institution. Such shifts are more easily absorbed if the institution and individual budget centres are in surplus. The more likely scenario, however, is that some budget centres will be in surplus whilst others will be in deficit. As discussed in the previous chapter, this leads to the issue of the extent to which cross-subsidies between surplus and deficit departments are to be accepted as a matter of policy or whether, over time, all budget centres will be expected to operate within the levels of income they attract. This decision is likely to influence the degree to which it is feasible to use a model for determining allocations. Clearly, the greater the disparity between surplus and deficit departments the more subjective judgement is required on the part of senior managers to ensure that budget centres have sufficient funds to operate whilst the institution as a whole remains in surplus. Thus, resource allocation models are most appropriate as determinants of allocation when the institution and individual budget centres are in surplus. On this basis, Figure 3.4 used in Chapter 3 to explain the three stage model may be expanded as shown in Figure 6.4.

Financial health should be seen not only in terms of surplus/ deficit but also in terms of stability. This can be difficult to achieve given periodic oscillations inherent in the funding councils' methodology. To achieve increasing levels of stability, institutions are placing more emphasis on securing non-funding-council income and are moving towards an increase in fixed-term appointments to match salary expenditure with known income streams. The significant factor here is that in any system that is reliant on significant levels of devolution, consistency of approach is important. To install a system of incentives raises expectations and affects institutional and individual behaviour patterns. To be forced to withdraw such incentives can create disillusionment within academic departments.

Priorities and preferences of key individuals

Despite the rhetoric of rationality that accompanies the introduction of devolution and formula-based approaches to resource allocation,

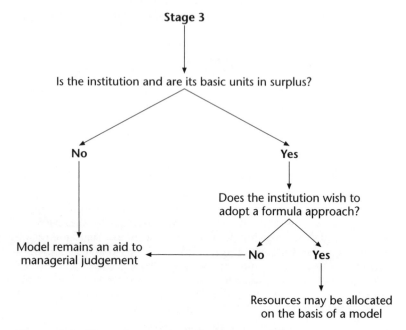

Figure 6.4   Uses of a resource allocation model

the system adopted is likely to be influenced by the priorities and preferences of a few key individuals, in particular the vice-chancellor or chief executive. It is here that chief executives can impose their style of management. Do they wish to exercise strong central direction with most key decisions requiring central management approval or do they prefer to set the framework centrally and encourage discretion lower down the institutional hierarchy? Are they comfortable with formulaic approaches or do they prefer the flexibility to exercise discretion and power through subjective judgement? On such personal factors are many key decisions taken.

Activities of powerful interest groups

The rhetoric accompanying the introduction of devolved, formula-based approaches is likely to be in terms of substituting a previous historical system based on decision by the chief executive, political manoeuvring and sub-unit power with a more rational system where outcomes are predictable and goals and purposes clear. There is evidence to suggest, however, that, notwithstanding this objective, the influence of power and political activity will remain. In the developmental stages in particular, micropolitical activity can influence the items to be devolved and the coefficients in the model with a consequential effect on the future financial health of a department. Thus, the political arguments may shift from the annual budget cycle to the formulation stage of the model, with long-term consequences for departmental allocations. In particular, the presence of deans or heads of department on the planning and resources committee introduces a tension between their managerial and representational roles. This is not to say, however, that such persons should not be involved, since wide ownership of the process is an important ingredient for success. It is necessary to recognize, however, that powerful interest groups can influence the decision-making process, notwithstanding the rhetoric of rationality.

Consequences

Institutional managers who embark on a process of greater devolution of financial responsibility to a departmental level need to be prepared for certain consequences at both institutional and departmental levels (Figure 6.5).

Institutional level

Cultural change

The introduction of a devolved, formula-based system of resource allocation is concerned as much with cultural change as with financial

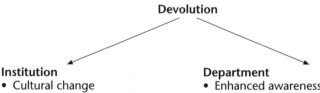

Devolution

Institution
- Cultural change
- Growth of internal markets
- Micropolitical activity
- Performance monitoring
- Implications for the planning process
- Interaction with departments
- Increased overhead costs

Department
- Enhanced awareness of environment
- Entrepreneurial opportunity
- Flexibility
- Development of strategic plans
- Increased workload
- Increased levels of concern
- Goal displacement

Figure 6.5   Consequences of devolution

management. Consequently, the introduction of devolved, formula-based models may unleash a period of cultural change that may not have been anticipated by the main proponents of change. In particular, an incentives-driven, formula-based approach, encouraging entrepreneurial activity can lead to a shift in power towards budget centres that are in surplus.

Growth of internal markets

The engendering of an entrepreneurial attitude is a key rationale of a formulaic approach, but the introduction of a scheme based on incentives may lead to the generation of an internal market with departments becoming inward looking. For instance, if the teaching element of departmental grants is determined according to student load figures, manipulation of the curriculum to withdraw the availability of an optional subject taught by a 'service' department can have a serious impact on that department's financial health, particularly a department which undertakes a significant amount of service teaching. Similarly, a department which has offered a common course with another department may find it financially advantageous to withdraw from such arrangements, leading to inefficiency in teaching and strains on space utilization. The extent to which such practices are accepted will depend upon the attitude of the senior management, particularly the chief executive, and views of the nature and culture of the institution. Such actions can be regarded either as a natural consequence of market forces and ignored, or as detrimental to collegiality in which case departmental actions will need to be constrained in the interest of the wider community.

Micropolitical activity

Any change in resource allocation systems is likely to generate micropolitical activity based on self-interest. This may be particularly evident when there is a rapid change from an historical, centralized system to a devolved, formula-based system without sufficient attention being paid to gaining wide acceptance and ownership of the new system. Evidence suggests that the reaction of heads of department will be to consider not the principles involved but the impact on their department. It is, therefore, important to proceed at a pace that ensures solid support. This pace could be largely influenced by the communication skills of the chief executive and other advocates of change. Moreover, there may be occasions when these protagonists need to pause to review developments if it appears, for instance, that practical constraints are hindering the implementation process.

Performance monitoring

Managers at all levels have to be capable of interpreting quantitative data. They have to be numerate, analytical and politically aware and conscious of the fact that the existence of such models may not in fact ease the decision-making process. Moreover, in those systems that employ a single financial model, the prime performance indicator becomes that of financial strength. The issue for senior managers is to balance this evaluative tool with that of academic reputation. The former is quantifiable; the latter, notwithstanding the existence of a multiplicity of performance indicators, remains more subjective. The balance is between financial viability and academic excellence and between departments in surplus wishing to expand and the well-being of the collegium which may mean protecting departments in deficit. In equating these different pressures, a devolved, formula-based approach is only one source of evaluation in the management and planning processes.

Implications for the planning process

Devolution to a departmental level can reinforce the culture of a strong departmental hierarchy, enhancing the power of departments and diminishing the role of the faculty or school in the planning process. When a department is the primary budgetary unit, there is likely to be a direct interaction between the department and the central resource allocation committee, for instance when central approval is required to fill a vacant post or to establish a new post. To establish the department as the primary budgetary unit when, historically, the faculty or school has had a coordinating role in the planning process is likely to have the effect of damaging consensus and reducing the role of the faculty/school in strategic planning. The priorities of surplus departments are likely to take precedence over more integrated faculty plans. Irrespective of other items that may be devolved, power and influence in the planning process are most likely to lie at the level which is responsible for salary expenditure. Thus, if there is an objective of building on a structure of strong departments, devolution of salary expenditure to the level of the department is likely to support that objective. On the other hand, if there is an objective of enhancing integration at a faculty/school level, devolution of salary costs to the level of a department will make that process more difficult.

The issue of where responsibility lies for salary costs is critical in determining the nature and extent of devolution. This is because a high percentage (perhaps over 70 per cent) of a budget centre's expenditure will relate to this item. Arguments in favour of devolution are that:

• it increases flexibility in the use of funds for those departments in surplus; and
• it forces departments in deficit to consider entrepreneurial approaches to ensure financial stability.

However, the effects can be:

• an increase in the levels of concern in those deficit departments where non-funding-council revenue is difficult to obtain; and
• a proliferation of posts in departments in surplus without sufficient integration and coordination between cognate departments.

It may, therefore, be suggested that salary costs should be devolved only if budget centres are of sufficient size that they can provide flexibility in the planning and budgetary processes. However, without devolution of salary costs, the sums for which a budget centre are responsible are much reduced, with adverse consequences for the degree of managerial flexibility that is feasible.

Some of the important issues that will have to be resolved in the design of a devolved system include:

• whether additional posts will be subject to central approval in view of the long-term financial commitment involved in their establishment;
• the extent to which staff promotion and discretionary payments will be subject to central approval; and
• whether actual salary costs will be charged to the budget centre or whether the charge will be based on a calculation of notional or average salaries for different salary bands.

In determining these issues a balance will have to be maintained between providing incentives for budget centres and maintaining a degree of institutional consensus and control. We return to these issues in Chapter 7. A possible framework based on the above analysis is shown in Figure 6.6.

Interaction with departments

As suggested elsewhere in this chapter, enhanced devolution brings with it a requirement for increased interaction between departmental managers and central administrators. For the latter, there is a

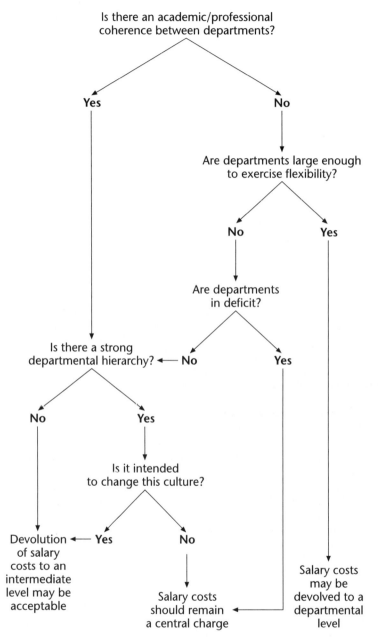

Figure 6.6   Devolution of salary costs

responsibility to adapt their approaches to provide a facilitating, supporting function which, in some cases, may require a physical relocation to the academic area they service.

Increased overhead costs

There is the danger that a devolved system might increase institutional overhead costs through an increase in monitoring and administrative tasks. Such dangers can be reduced by giving attention to the prerequisites and determinants outlined earlier in this chapter, but in the light of each institution's circumstances senior managers will need to consider whether the introduction of such systems will be cost effective. The objective will be to encourage an entrepreneurial culture which will lead to an increase in income, but if the cost of operating such schemes outweighs the net increase in income then the goals of the institution will not be enhanced.

Departmental level

Chapter 8 focuses on the management of financial resources from a departmental perspective, so we shall not explore the issues in any depth here. In summary, however, enhanced devolution accompanied by a formula-based approach increases the need for managerial activity at a departmental level and can gave rise to contradictory pressures. On the one hand, positive consequences might be seen as:

- an enhanced awareness of the external environment;
- the opportunity to benefit from entrepreneurial activity. The introduction of a formula-based model demonstrating how a department's income is generated, combined with a decentralized system, offers departments a more direct incentive to save and an encouragement to undertake activities that will generate additional income in the knowledge that a share of that income will be allocated to the department;
- increased flexibility and a more effective use of resources through the ability to vire between different heads of expenditure and to carry forward surpluses; and
- the opportunity to develop strategic plans. As seen in Chapter 5, a formula-based model can encourage the formulation of departmental plans in consultation with those involved with the planning process in the central administration, thereby bringing, through the existence of a planning model, a degree of consistency between institutional and departmental aspirations.

On the other hand, devolution can:

* increase the workload of academic and administrative staff, thereby increasing the overhead costs of the institution;
* increase the levels of concern for some heads of department. For a thriving department in surplus, the certainty of an incentives-driven, formula-based approach with the expectation of continuity in the method of funding may have considerable advantages, but for a deficit department with limited income-generating potential and with a head of department who is not numerate, the added concern of having to understand the consequences and coefficients of the formula, together with the need to reconcile figures with the central administration and to keep departmental accounts, can give rise to considerable concern; and
* lead to a fear that some members of the academic staff will be diverted from their primary role of teaching and research with consequential goal displacement.

Conclusion

This chapter has provided analysis and frameworks to aid decisions on the nature of resource allocation systems to be adopted in institutions of higher education. Those frameworks incorporated:

* the uses of the formula model in terms of an aid to managerial judgement and as a determinant of allocations;
* the extent of devolution of financial decision making, including the ability to carry forward surpluses (and deficits) and the ability to vire between budget heads. It was suggested that a crucial issue was the extent to which salary costs remained a central charge or were devolved to a budget centre level;
* prerequisites to ensure that any system of enhanced devolution provided an effective management system;
* determinants which might influence the nature of the resource allocation system adopted by any particular institution; and
* consequences to be anticipated at both institutional and departmental levels.

Chapters 4 to 6 have focused on mechanisms for the allocation of income. By setting expenditure against those income figures, a surplus or deficit for each component part of the institution provides valuable information for senior managers. It is to the monitoring of this expenditure that we turn in the next chapter.

7

MONITORING

Brian Lewis

Introduction

The need for monitoring

Theory generally states that increased delegation leads to greater efficiency and better staff motivation, and it is this concept which has prompted higher education institutions to delegate. Consequently, monitoring at the level of detail involved in schemes of delegation has related to internally driven needs. Increasingly, however, there is external intervention which enforces the same level of monitoring even in higher education institutions without extensive delegation. To satisfy government and its agencies, proper use of public funds and a search for value for money must be constantly demonstrable.

> Everyone believes in delegation. But it needs clear rules to become productive. It requires that the delegated task be clearly defined, that there are mutually understood goals and mutually agreed on deadlines . . . Delegation further requires that delegators follow up. They rarely do – they think they have delegated, and that's it. But they are still accountable for performance.
>
> (Drucker 1990)

It is that accountability for performance combined with the importance of accountability for public funds that should drive the monitoring process.

Any opposition by senior management to increased delegation may be based on a fear of loss of control; opposition by line managers may be based on a fear of a greatly increased workload or of lack of expertise. Both problems can be resolved by careful implementation and effective monitoring. Peters and Waterman (1982: 318) describe the benefits of simultaneous loose–tight properties within organizations: 'in essence the co-existence of firm central direction and maximum individual autonomy', and provide comfort to senior managers that a properly implemented process of delegation, combined with the retention of tight control over corporate strategic direction, provides a framework for the development of excellence in organizations.

If we accept that delegation is a tool used by managers to channel the powers and abilities of individuals in order to get things done, then it is clear that, in so doing, managers must monitor the activities of those individuals in order to maintain accountability. Delegation is about getting done what the organization wants done, not what the individual wants done. The challenge is to allow maximum delegated flexibility whilst ensuring that information systems and reporting procedures are sufficiently robust to provide a monitoring framework which guards against the organization being deflected from its strategic path and ensures that there are no surprises. 'Devolution of financial responsibility forces the academic operating units to face up to the hard choices which have to be made' (Williams 1992: 144), but they should not be cut adrift: monitoring should be a means of support as well as control.

However, it would be wrong to assume that detailed monitoring is necessary only because of delegation. The period since the early 1980s has been one of turbulent change in the UK higher education system with a critically important factor being 'the move from opaquely constructed block grants to a multi-stranded transparent funding system' (Bourn 1994a: 23). As a result, there is extensive external pressure to improve the quality of monitoring information in all institutions which stems from the demand for public accountability. There is a range of issues to be addressed:

- There is a general requirement to account properly for the use of public funds.
- Teaching grant and research grant are discrete funding streams which should be accounted for separately.
- Public funds should not be used to subsidize commercial operations.
- Catering and residence provision within institutions is expected to be self-financing.
- There is a general requirement on governing bodies and principals to secure the efficient and effective use of resources.

All these requirements exist regardless of the extent of delegation. Institutions which do not have suitable systems in place can fall foul of various external monitoring agencies.

Such demands for accountability have a cost, and institutions, rather than simply responding to external demands, should seek to maximize the benefits to themselves by using the information and the systems generated as an aid to the improvement of their efficiency and competitiveness within an environment where funding is likely to continue to reduce in real terms.

Some risks of devolution

Devolution carries with it some risks, but efficient monitoring can minimize those risks. The most obvious risk is that budgets will be overspent; thus efficient management information systems and effective monitoring are prerequisites of the introduction of a scheme of delegation.

There is also a risk that resources may be inappropriately used; for example, where staffing budgets are delegated, there may be a temptation to appoint 'cheap', inexperienced staff as a means of diverting funds to other uses. But good human resource management policies and effective quality control should guard against such actions.

Loss of strategic direction may be a risk within an organization which fails properly to monitor and control a scheme of delegation. This is potentially serious and needs to be guarded against as it may be more insidious and difficult to spot than the simpler issues of overspend or misuse of resources. If managers see delegation as a means of following their own paths rather than those defined by the corporate whole then problems will arise. To quote Bourn (1994a: 19): 'the main concern would almost certainly be whether the university can maintain its integrity as an institution if resources and responsibilities have been devolved so fully to faculties. Will it become the battleground for deans acting like feuding robber barons?' Again, effective monitoring and control and application of the 'simultaneous loose–tight' principles outlined above will prevent such a situation arising. There is a need to counter 'centrifugal forces tending towards fragmentation' (Bourn 1994a: 23), and the more extensive the delegation the greater the centrifugal forces.

One may argue that for a scheme of delegation, control and monitoring of budgets to be effective there must be a perception that the budget itself is effective. If it is to operate as an effective management tool a budget should be fair, participative, even-handed, reasonable, cognitive of the real environment, supportive and supported, and committed (i.e. guaranteed) (CIMA 1996). If attention is paid to each of these factors during the budget-setting process itself then the risks associated with delegation can be minimized. Participation in the process by those receiving delegated budgets is more likely to produce a perception of effectiveness than is delivery of a *fait accompli*.

This chapter deals primarily with monitoring and control in the routine sense where a central service, usually the finance office, prepares reports on a regular basis to provide information for both budget-holders and senior management in order that income and expenditure may be controlled against budgets. However, when designing schemes of delegation, institutions should also be aware of the need to ensure that strategic control is maintained.

The regulatory framework

All publicly funded higher education institutions are accountable to their funding agencies and governments (Figure 7.1). In the UK, the monitoring is carried out by each national funding council. In a relatively short chapter it is possible to give only indications of the relevant statutes and regulations. The regulatory framework described here is specific to the UK but the underlying principles will be applicable to any publicly funded system. All the rules apply to a greater or lesser extent to the operation of schemes of delegation. Senior managers designing schemes should always be aware of the detailed regulations which apply. Those in receipt of delegated budgets should understand that the internal rules they have to work with are, to an extent, in response to the strict external controls which exist, even though the concept of institutional autonomy may sit uncomfortably within such a framework.

Relevant legislation

The key items of legislation relevant to monitoring are the Education Reform Act 1988 and the Further and Higher Education Act 1992. It is the combination of the provisions of these Acts which created the single higher education system which exists today in the UK and created the funding councils which have responsibility for both the funding and the financial monitoring of all higher education institutions.

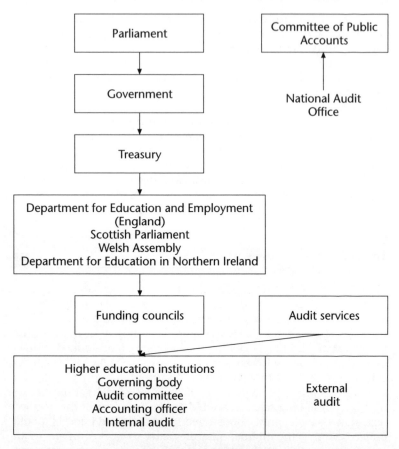

Figure 7.1   The regulatory framework of UK higher education

Responsibilities which cannot be delegated ('strategy and solvency')

The constitution and powers of the governing body are specified in the charter and statutes of the pre-1992 universities and, in the case of the post-1992 universities and colleges, in the Education Reform Act 1988 and the Further and Higher Education Act 1992. The post-1992 universities and colleges also have instruments and articles of government which specify the responsibilities of their governing bodies. The strategic and financial responsibilities, as summarized by the Committee of University Chairmen (CUC 1995) and Higher Education Funding Council for Wales (HEFCW 1995), include:

- the determination of the educational character and mission of the institution and the oversight of its activities;
- approving annual operating plans and operating budgets which should reflect the institution's strategic plan;
- the effective and efficient use of resources, the solvency of the institution and the safeguarding of its assets;
- approving annual estimates of income and expenditure;
- receiving and approving the annual accounts;
- ensuring the existence and integrity of financial control systems;
- the appointment, grading, assignment, suspension, dismissal and determination of the pay and conditions of service of the principal, the clerk to the governing body and the holders of such other senior posts as the governing body may determine in consultation with the principal; and
- setting a framework for the pay and conditions of other staff.

Financial memorandum

A financial memorandum between the funding councils and individual institutions defines the rules which govern their relationship. In particular, it emphasizes the importance of accountability for the proper use of public funds and the fact that the governing body has ultimate responsibility for monitoring the institution.

Audit Code of Practice

The financial memorandum between the funding councils and the relevant government departments requires the councils to issue a code of practice governing institutions' audit arrangements (see, for example, Welsh Office 1996: para. 4.9). The code is comprehensive and much of the content is, in fact, mandatory.

Statement of recommended practice

A statement of recommended practice (SORP), as approved by the Accounting Standards Board, provides guidance on the precise format of institutions' final accounts (SORP 2000). However, this document, as it relates only to the aggregate financial statements, is of limited relevance to schemes of delegation.

External audit

The Further and Higher Education Act 1992 requires that all institutions appoint suitably qualified external auditors. The funding councils' Audit Code of Practice (HEFCW 1999) states that the role of external audit is to report on the financial statements and to carry out such an examination of the financial statements and underlying records and control systems as necessary to form an opinion on the statements. That is basically the same role that external audit performs in any organization, be it private or public sector. However, the code of practice goes on to emphasize that the audit of public funds is different from audit in the commercial sector and auditors are required to go beyond the usual statement that an institution's accounts represent a true and fair view. It is required that they should also state whether funding received from the funding councils has been properly applied for the purpose provided and in accordance with the financial memorandum. On that basis one may expect external auditors to take some interest in a scheme of delegation in order that they may satisfy themselves that adequate controls exist to guard against inappropriate use of public funds.

Funding council audit

The chief executives of the funding councils are designated as the councils' accounting officers and, as such, are responsible to parliament for ensuring that the uses to which the councils put funds received from government are consistent with the purposes for which the funds were given and comply with the conditions attached to them. As the funding councils' chief executives are responsible to parliament, they need to be satisfied that institutions have appropriate arrangements for financial management and accounting and that they use funds consistently with the purposes for which they were given. In order to discharge their monitoring responsibilities, the funding councils periodically review the financial health of institutions by reference to a range of information including the annual accounts, financial forecasts and audit reports. This review results in institutions' being classified as either satisfactory, marginal or unsatisfactory (at risk).

An institution is classified as unsatisfactory if it faces immediate financial difficulties. Marginal institutions are those considered to be facing short-term financial difficulties which are currently not serious or where there may be financial difficulties in the future. There is little effect in practice in being downgraded from satisfactory to marginal apart from some increased pressure from the councils to rectify any perceived weaknesses. Classification as 'at risk' leads to a significant increase in the level of funding council monitoring, including a requirement for submission of monthly progress reports and audit certification of the accuracy and reasonableness of financial forecasts. It should be noted, however, that the reference to possible difficulties in the future within the marginal classification provides the funding council with an opportunity to make its views known to a governing body if it is dissatisfied with any significant aspect of control or monitoring.

Whilst the funding councils generally promote delegation as good management practice, they also expect to see structured and effective monitoring processes in support of schemes of delegation.

Internal control requirements

An institution embarking on a scheme of delegation will need to determine its own internal control processes whilst being aware that there are laid down minimum requirements for monitoring.

Responsibilities of the governing body

As outlined above, the governing body is responsible for factors sometimes summarized as 'strategy and solvency'. In discharging those responsibilities it is reasonable to expect the governing body to require the provision of monitoring information on a regular basis. This should be in a form determined by the governing body itself but, increasingly, there is external pressure to define what should be provided. Current initiatives on costing and pricing, as described later in this chapter, are likely to increase governing body interest in costs at departmental level.

Audit committee

The Audit Code of Practice requires each institution to have an audit committee with extensive responsibilities for monitoring which include appointing the internal and external auditors and ensuring that their recommendations are properly considered and acted upon.

Responsibilities of the designated accounting officer

The principal, vice-chancellor or equivalent is designated as accounting officer under funding council rules and as such acts as the institution's chief executive. The accounting officer is required to advise the governing body if it is in breach of the financial memorandum and is obliged to inform the funding council if this advice is disregarded. In the event of problems arising, it is the accounting officer, not the governing body, who may be required to appear before the Public Accounts Committee (PAC). However, it should be noted that, in practice, recent National Audit Office (NAO) reports and the subsequent PAC hearings (notably relating to Swansea Institute of Higher Education (NAO 1997), Southampton Institute (NAO 1998), Gwent Tertiary College (NAO 1999a) and Halton College (NAO 1999b)) have not required the accounting officer to attend (in these cases the accounting officer had resigned) but they have been heavily criticized. The accounting officer may therefore run the risk of being tried and convicted in his or her absence with little opportunity to offer any defence.

Financial regulations

The financial memorandum and the Audit Code of Practice require all institutions to ensure that they have sound systems of internal financial management and control. Grant can be withheld if the funding council is unable to satisfy itself that properly documented procedures are in place and institutions are expected to have financial regulations which govern the conduct of all their financial affairs. A model set of regulations has been published by the Chartered Institute of Public Finance and Accounting (CIPFA 1996). However, the financial regulations of an institution are normally drafted to cover only the broad principles of financial control. They should include provision to permit a scheme of delegated financial management to exist and spell out the general rules under which it may operate, but the detail of the scheme should be contained within a supplementary set of comprehensive rules and procedures.

Internal audit

The Audit Code of Practice includes a mandatory requirement that every institution must have an effective internal audit function. The internal audit service is required to cover the whole internal control system of the institution and must produce an annual report to the governing body and the institution's accounting officer. Internal auditors will take a keen interest in delegated financial management and should be involved in the design process of the scheme. Their strategic audit plan should ensure adequate review subsequent to implementation of the scheme.

Current UK national initiatives to promote good practice

It may be seen from the above that although, in theory, higher education institutions are autonomous bodies, this state exists only within a requirement to be publicly accountable. The extent of control and regulation is extensive and financial audit of one form or another is an everyday experience for higher education institutions. On top of this come the attentions paid by the European Court of Auditors and its agencies for institutions which receive European Community grants and the attentions of agencies such as the Inland Revenue and Customs and Excise which apply to all organizations.

There is also considerable activity sector-wide in the UK to promote the funding councils' view of good practice. However, it is becoming increasingly common in reality for these initiatives to be mandatory in practice and institutional autonomy is, arguably, reducing. The key initiatives at present are as follows.

Corporate governance and risk management

A cornerstone of recent recommendations on corporate governance, notably the 1999 Combined Code of Practice of the Committee of Corporate Governance (the Turnbull Report) is that companies should carry out full risk assessments which take account of the entire internal control system (ICAEW 1999: 1). In brief, companies need to have in place procedures to:

- establish business objectives;
- identify the risks associated with them;
- agree on the appropriate control processes to address these risks; and
- set up a system to implement and regularly monitor these.

The Combined Code describes practices expected in companies listed on the London Stock Exchange but these are transferable to the public sector, and the funding councils consider that they represent best practice which higher education institutions should strive to replicate. The exercise is clearly wide-ranging and potentially very complex and time consuming but the growing likelihood that higher education institutions will be required to include an audited corporate governance statement in their annual accounts makes such an exercise essential (CIPFA 1999). This risk assessment will impact on delegation as it will involve a fundamental review of all resource allocation, budgeting, budgetary control and accounting procedures.

Space management

The National Audit Office (1994: 6) stated that: 'institutions need to consider whether existing space is being used efficiently. There is scope for institutions to extend the practice of attributing the cost of space occupied where appropriate'. The view is that charging for space will improve space utilization as it will encourage budget-holders to relinquish surplus accommodation held. Funding council surveys of space utilization indicate levels as low as 20 per cent and less in some institutions and pressure is being put on all institutions to carry out detailed space utilization surveys with a view to increasing the figure across the sector to at least 30 per cent.

Costing and pricing

'The new imperative for British universities is that planning must now be justified on financial as well as academic grounds. University leaders and planners must uncover the exact costs of each of their operations' (Temple and Whitchurch 1994: 18). Until recently the key guidance on costing was contained in the Hanham Report (1988). In recent years, pressure to reduce reliance on public funding has grown and institutions have been encouraged to obtain income from non-government sources, either by recruiting full-cost overseas students or by commercial work. This has resulted in a need to ensure that provision is accurately costed in order that adequate prices may be charged. There has also been growing concern that the real costs of teaching, research and consultancy may not be fully appreciated, with the result that funding may be diverted from the intended area. Consequently, there are now two major initiatives to improve the quality of costing information in higher education institutions:

1 The Costing and Pricing Initiative, coordinated by the Joint Costing and Pricing Strategy Group, aims to ensure that institutions develop institution-wide costing and pricing strategies which take account of the full cost of operations and 'integrate the academic and financial management processes at the level of primary decision making' (Joint Funding Councils 1997).

2 The Transparency Review of Research set up by the UK research councils was initially focused on the research-intensive institutions and aimed to ensure that the costs of teaching and research are properly separated. However, the review extends to all institutions which will be required to have systems for full transparency in place by 2003.

Both of these initiatives take practical considerations into account, recognize the problems associated with costing and overhead allocation in higher education, and aim to arrive, by means of simple systems, at a set of reasonable costs rather than a complex system which may give spurious accuracy.

Once these systems are in place, and governing bodies become aware of the implications of the information produced, one may expect that schemes of delegation will fall under increasing scrutiny and criticism, especially in circumstances where cross-subsidy between budget centres exists as a result of internal resource allocation procedures being significantly different from the assumptions underlying the external funding mechanism, an issue covered briefly later in this chapter.

Joint Procurement Policy and Strategy Group

Procurement of goods and services is a high profile issue within all public sector organizations and the National Audit Office and the funding councils have taken great interest in the subject in higher education. The need to demonstrate that serious efforts are made to obtain value for money is sharply focused on this subject. The Joint Procurement Policy and Strategy Group is an organization set up by the funding councils to provide advice on purchasing in higher education. The guidance it produces is voluminous and beyond the scope of this book, other than in the sense that schemes of delegation need to recognize that this guidance exists, that the funding councils expect it to be followed, and that monitoring and control systems need to ensure that budget-holders do not act in a manner likely to lead to criticism. It is not, therefore, sufficient simply to monitor expenditure against budgets and to report on that basis alone. Central monitoring procedures also need to ensure that purchases by budget-holders are supported by evidence, such as competitive quotes, in order that it may be demonstrated that value for money is being obtained. There are also other issues which need to be carefully considered and implemented if they are not to be seen as attempts to limit excessively the delegated powers of budget-holders. Bulk purchasing is one case in point. For example, where computing equipment is purchased by budget-holders, it is highly likely that a coordinated approach which combines a number of small-value purchases into one large purchase will lead to the unit price of the equipment reducing.

'Effective financial management'

In 1998, the funding councils issued guidance on effective financial management which is not mandatory at present but is clearly taken into account by the funding councils' audit services when they carry out institutional reviews. The guidance also impacts on the work of internal auditors. The guidance is designed to allow members of governing bodies, heads of institutions and senior managers to test the effectiveness of financial management arrangements at their institutions, to ensure that they are appropriate and robust. The test should be based on a series of self-challenge questions and the head of the institution should take account of the outcomes in any assurances given to the governing body (HEFCE 1998). The checklist includes a section on the management of resources and regards delegation and comprehensive monitoring to be sound management practice.

National Audit Office value for money studies and institutional reports

A number of reports have been issued by the National Audit Office in recent years on issues throughout the further and higher education sectors and on problems within specific institutions. The Public Accounts Committee hearings which have considered these reports have been highly critical of management and governance within institutions and of failures in the funding councils' monitoring procedures. Furthermore, the Committee has expressed concerns that the problems identified within specific institutions may exist in many other institutions. As a result, the funding councils are now issuing these reports to institutions with a requirement that senior managers take account of the recommendations, review the institution's status in relationship to them and report the findings to the institution's audit committee.

The Public Accounts Committee's criticisms of the management of overseas operations at Swansea and Southampton Institutes and the Training Shop at Gwent Tertiary College are examples of delegation being allowed, by governors and senior managers, to go too far in terms of independence. Peters and Waterman (1982) refer to the concept of 'sticking to the knitting' and point out the dangers of uncontrolled diversification which departs from the core strategy of a business: this too is particularly relevant in these cases.

All these initiatives may lead one to suggest that we live in an over-regulated world, but it is difficult to argue against the basic principle that public funds should be safeguarded. However, these requirements apply to all institutions, large or small, and the cost of compliance, especially for the small, can be significant.

Accounting issues ■

The information problem

'Information itself is not the scarce resource in organizations. Advanced information technology provides managers with bundles of data to assist in making decisions. We live in a world that drenches us with information. The scarce resource is the processing capacity to attend to information' (Robbins 1990: 110). This information problem can act as a significant deterrent to the introduction of a scheme of financial delegation for the following reasons:

- Those receiving delegated powers will demand information to assist them in the preparation and control of budgets.
- Those at the centre are likely to demand information to assist them in monitoring the delegated budgets to ensure that control is being maintained.

The demands of one group are likely to be different from the demands of the other and, consequently, the additional workload placed on the finance, computing and other central services can be heavy.

However, even if a good information system exists in an institution, there is one potential problem which may be insurmountable without a major culture change and that is the issue of 'information is power'. In some organizations a culture exists which requires that information is 'owned' by senior management and is used as a weapon of control. In such an environment, information, even of a relatively trivial nature, is 'protected and controlled as a personal asset, fed out selectively to enhance power' (Turner 1992: 2). Such organizations are unlikely even to consider the introduction of delegated financial management.

Where delegated management is introduced, feedback of information is particularly important to the success of the scheme. Behavioural research on information feedback has shown that lack of knowledge about current performance can have a significantly negative effect on motivation and morale as well as on future performance. It is also observed that the absence of, or delays in, the provision of feedback information tends to be accompanied by high hostility and low confidence in a scheme, whereas a high level of feedback information tends to be accompanied by a supportive attitude and confidence in the scheme. It is apparent, therefore, that for delegation to be successful, a good information system is of special concern in the design of the scheme.

Accountants designing such an information feedback system need to guard against the danger of assuming that a system based on breaking up the aggregated information which has, historically, been held at the centre will suffice. At first this will probably be the case, and simple weekly or monthly reports giving details of actual spend and commitments will be adequate. However, as the scheme develops, and interest increases, budget-holders are likely to require more sophisticated information as an indication of relative levels of performance. From the outset, therefore, it needs to be recognized that the demand for information could be large and systems should be designed to be sufficiently detailed and flexible in their coding structures to allow detailed management accounting information and performance indicators to be developed. This process will impose a workload on finance and computing staff who will need to design the systems required to amalgamate financial and non-financial data in order to obtain the required information whilst bearing in mind that 'the budgetary control reports must provide sufficient information to enable budget holders to isolate the nature of variances from the budget but must not contain so much information that the recipient is overwhelmed' (Jones and Pendlebury 1996: 30).

According to Hopwood (1984: 178): 'The selective visibility which accounting gives to organizational actions and outcomes can play an important role in influencing what comes to be seen as problematic, possible, desirable and significant'. If this is true, then, within the organizational culture of higher education institutions, which are frequently viewed as anarchic (Cohen and March 1974), there may be resistance to the improvement of accounting if this produces information which can be used against specific groups within an institution. There may also be elements within the organization, especially in the case of traditional 'old' universities, where staff believe that 'the assessment movement is an attempt by philistines to control the content and manner of instruction' (Newton 1992: 12). The obvious fear is that production of accounting information will expose those areas which are inefficient and increase the threat of closure or other action. That fear may be well founded for those within threatened areas, but it is the health of the corporate whole which should concern senior managers of institutions. The accounting process should be used as a part of the decision-making process and be integrated with other techniques. The key danger to avoid is the politicization of the process, where manipulation of the methodology is used to create 'answers' which suit particular agenda and are presented as irrefutable facts. The role of management accounting should be to inform in a neutral manner, even if that provokes painful decisions. Useful guidance is offered by the University of Texas on principles guiding institutional programme closure, relocation or reorganization where the process should: '1. Introduce into the discussion the views of the administration, faculty, staff, students and community with adequate representation from affected constituencies; and 2. Be open and public. A rationale should be published for all decisions' (University of Texas 1996: 14). This fully recognizes the wide range of stakeholders involved in higher education institutions.

Chart of accounts

An institution's chart of accounts provides the basic building-blocks of all its financial reporting procedures. It is more commonly known to staff outside the finance office by some description such as 'the financial coding list'. Within a scheme of delegation it is essential that the chart is sufficiently detailed to provide adequate management information to budget centre managers and to provide meaningful monitoring data, both at a detailed and an aggregate level, to senior management. The usual way of providing this capability is by ensuring that the chart of accounts has a hierarchical structure which matches the organizational structure of the institution. The concept is best described by an example such as the following structure operated by the Australian National University (2000).

Each accounting transaction bears an account code indicating type of funding, responsibility centre details and type of transaction. The overall form of the code is:

A SS DDD SD SD GG AAAA SA

All fields in the code are alphanumerical:

A Ledger Segment. This is a required single alpha character that represents the segment of the ledger.
S Schools. This is two required digits representing a university budget or business unit.
D Department. Three required digits representing a subset of the school level, such as an academic department or other responsibility centre.
SD Sub-department. An optional field of two digits to provide lower-order reporting within a department where required, e.g. for academic activities and pursuits, special purpose funds.
G Group. An optional field of two digits to provide lower-order reporting within a sub-department where required, e.g. for project accounting and consolidations.
A Natural Account. A required four-digit code indicating type of transaction. (In the UK the natural code would be most commonly described as the subjective code.)
SA Sub-account. An optional field of one digit to provide lower-order reporting within a natural account.

When all the required fields of a School–Department–Account combination are correctly entered, a valid account code is formed. For example, R43020——5208- which gives:

R   Recurrent
43   Research School of Physical Sciences
020   Department of Nuclear Physics
5208 Electronic and electrical materials

This example is well suited to a scheme of delegation as the information required by senior management for monitoring purposes is provided by mandatory fields within the code, whereas the optional fields permit budget centre managers to tailor the coding information to suit their own local needs.

Management accounting needs

Drury (1996: 4) distinguishes between management and financial accounting in the following way: 'Management accounting is concerned with the provision of information to people within the organization to help them to make better decisions, whereas financial accounting is concerned with the provision of information to external parties outside the organization'.

Johnson and Kaplan's critiques *Relevance Lost* (1987) and Johnson's *Relevance Regained* (1994) refer to the fact that, historically, financial accounting has been at the fore in organizations. This is certainly true of higher education institutions, where there has always been a need, first and foremost, to provide information which satisfies the paymaster – the government – on behalf of the taxpayer. However, as pressure grows to improve internal efficiency, then management accounting increases in importance.

> The outcomes of the management accounting process are assessed in terms of the value they add to an organization, judged from the perspective of users of the outcomes. Thus, the accountability of the management accounting function is outwardly directed, to organizational participants served by the function.
>
> (International Federation of Accountants 1998)

Given that fact, it is reasonable to assume that the management accounting process will be more useful if the organizational participants to be served have some input to its design. This is particularly true of higher education institutions which tend to have more democratic styles than many other organizations, with the result that staff expect to be consulted on a wide range of issues. Fortunately, 'in many ways, the unique impulse in higher education to consult broadly, to engage in critical exchange, and to respect diverse opinions is the wellspring of our industry's ability to renew itself continually' (Jonas *et al.* 1997).

Writing on the subject of the serious financial difficulties at University College, Cardiff, in the late-1980s, Shattock (1988: 12) stated that:

> The real lesson to be learned from the Cardiff experience is that organizational culture is a crucial element in the management of an institution. Good financial management is dependent on a positive organizational culture and an ineffective organizational culture will not easily be changed quickly either by removing a few senior individuals, or by external exhortation through the medium of efficiency reports or governmental pressure. An effective organizational culture needs to be developed and maintained over many years: there are no short cuts.

However, in the case of recent, well publicized cases in the UK, the reaction to the identification of problems has been to remove a few senior individuals, report publicly on their inefficiencies and, by means of funding council exhortation, require all institutions to examine their own practices.

Institutions require an integrated system which features:

For cost centre/operating units:

- Payments and commitments to date by operating units and projects.
- Payments to date by type of expenditure and supplier and discounts obtained.
- Uncommitted resources to date.
- Other returns to users' requirements.

For intermediate levels of responsibility:

- Summary reports of unit financial operations related to budgets.
- Aggregated financial reports for the area of responsibility.

For high-level responsibility:

- Annual first and revised estimates in total and by appropriate sectors of responsibility.
- Summary financial reports related to budget in total and by sectors of responsibility.
- Cash flow report and forecast.
- Performance analyses of relevant indicators such as discounts received, frequency and volume of purchases by type, etc.

And on specific budget centre responsibility:

- Each budget centre should prepare an annual plan including a budget covering all the expenditures for which it is responsible. When this has been approved or amended by the planning and resources committee and council, the centre should be monitored and held fully accountable for the plan's fulfilment.
- Each budget centre should be given as much delegated authority for administering its plan as is consistent with the procedures and regulations laid down above, and within the requirements of internal audit.
- Where there are intermediate authorities within the budgetary line they should hold the primary budget centres responsible for the performance and themselves account to the planning and resources committee.

Figure 7.2 A simple delegated management accounting scheme

The Jarratt Report of 1985 outlined various management accounting needs in universities. These are summarized in Figure 7.2.

Figure 7.2 represents a simple recipe for a delegated scheme. However, it should also be noted that: 'The cost of the measurement system should not be unreasonable. In other words, the benefits from adopting the measurement system should be greater than the costs of operating the system. Also, the measurement unit should be understandable to the users. Finally, the basis of the measurement should be relevant to the decision' (Drury 1996: 6). Avoidance of overcomplexity is important; Bourn (1993), Burnett *et al.* (1994), Groves *et al.* (1994), Scapens *et al.* (1994), Tomkins and Mawditt (1994) all highlight the considerable complexities which can emerge from an exercise which at first examination would appear to be fairly simple. Practical implementation needs to be focused on developing a system which suits the needs of the institution without going overboard in terms of sophistication which is expensive to maintain.

Commitment accounting

The Jarratt Report referred in 1985 to the need to provide details of both payments and commitments (for example, goods ordered but not yet paid for). Perhaps surprisingly, the National Audit Office reported in 1994 that 46 per cent of higher education institutions did not include details of outstanding orders/commitments in budget reports. It is suggested here that the risk of serious problems developing in a scheme of delegation will be greatly increased if institutions do not have the capability to record and report on the level of outstanding commitments. However, commercial accounting packages frequently do not provide such a facility and institutions may need to change their software or develop alternative arrangements for recording commitments. Both are potentially expensive actions which should be taken into account when considering the introduction of a delegation scheme, but where the main accounting software is not capable of recording commitments then alternative, local, spreadsheet-based systems can fairly easily be introduced.

Charging for staff: average or actual salaries?

Staffing represents the largest single element of cost for higher education institutions. There are issues related to staff costs which can impact adversely on a scheme of delegation if budget centre managers are given total control over staffing decisions, especially if the institution experiences high staff turnover. Many budget centre managers will view delegation as a means of freeing discretionary cash to spend on previously unaffordable items. One means of doing this would be to seek to appoint staff on low grades or low salary points within grades. Such an action can have two potentially damaging effects if carried too far:

1 It raises questions of quality if the staff appointed are 'cheap' owing to their lack of experience or qualifications.
2 It may cause problems regarding issues of equal pay if staff within one part of an organization are being remunerated at a level significantly below staff elsewhere with similar responsibilities.

One means of reducing the risk of this happening is to charge staff costs to devolved budgets at the average cost, by grade, within the institution as a whole. The budget centre manager is thus discouraged from 'buying cheap' when appointing staff as it will have little impact on the charge he will receive. (There is, of course, the opposite problem that the budget centre managers may then choose to appoint very well qualified and experienced staff to all posts with the result that the institutional average cost will gradually rise.)

The option for budget centre managers to make savings by deleting posts and increasing efficiency will remain. If this approach is adopted it will make the accounting process more complex as staff costs will need to be pooled and charges to departments made from that pool. If the pool is to be kept in balance then the average costs need to be recalculated regularly and great care needs to be taken to ensure that poor updating does not lead to a position where recharged salaries are lower than the true average: a situation which could permit deficits to arise.

For many institutions, an averaging method will prove to be too cumbersome to operate, in which case risk can be minimized by ensuring that budget centre managers are prevented from taking final decisions on staff appointments without consulting central personnel staff. It should be noted that the University of Bath, which has an extensively delegated approach, permitted schools to appoint which staff they wished, but this was subject to the terms and standards to be applied to staff remaining under central control (Tomkins and Mawditt 1994: 25) and subject to schools' 'demonstrating that both academic and financial viability of their three-year plans would be maintained' (p. 29).

Charging for central services

The *Good Management Practice Guide* issued by the National Advisory Body for Local Authority Higher Education (NAB 1986), referred to the need to devolve responsibility to faculties or departments and also to recharge central services to the academic units. Such a policy of recharging encourages critical examination of all an institution's costs and avoids the risk of accusations that those at the point of course delivery are being squeezed whilst those at the 'centre' are protected. However, the difficulties associated with developing overhead recharge mechanisms should not be underestimated. There are numerous ways of recharging overheads (see, for example, Bourn 1994b; Scapens *et al.* 1994) and all can be perceived to be both right and wrong in equal measures. One should also bear in mind that there is a difference between charging overheads for purposes of delegated control, which can be restricted to certain elements, and charging for costing purposes which, under the new approaches encouraged by the Transparency Review and the Costing and Pricing Initiative requirements, has to be carried out in full.

There will always be an element of arbitrariness in whichever approach is adopted and this is one area which provides a rich seam of arguments, disputes and opportunities for confusion. If we consider three specific areas the problems can be illustrated:

- *Space.* Charging for accommodation space has been introduced by a number of institutions, partly as a means of responding to the entreaties from government agencies to improve space utilization which are mentioned earlier in this chapter. There are considerable advantages if useful space is released or if utilization is improved but the system will fail if it simply leads to frantic attempts to dispose of broom cupboards and disused corners. The charging mechanism itself can be complex: for example, how much additional weight should be given to a square metre of engineering space compared with a square metre of lecture theatre?
- *Senior management and central administration.* No one wants to pay for these, so all methods of charging are unfair!
- *Computing, libraries and learning resources.* Charge by actual usage, by student numbers, by weighted student numbers?

A simplified approach is not to charge out overheads at all but to keep all such costs under central control funded by 'top-sliced' resources. This can reduce the incentive to examine critically a significant proportion of an institution's expenditure and still leaves the problem of determining what is a fair top-slice. Williams (1990: 24) describes a range of approaches to resource allocation and these are worth repeating here:

Administratively a higher education institution consists essentially of a central bureaucracy, a number of centrally provided services and a varied collection of more or less specialised operating units consisting of faculties, departments and research centres.

Even this simplified structure allows for eight distinct internal resource allocation procedures:

1 All income goes to the centre and expenditure decisions, both strategic and operational are taken there.
2 Income is received, strategic priorities are established and some operational decisions, usually those that have long term implications such as recruitment of staff, are taken centrally; but routine expenditure decisions are taken in the operating units.
3 Income received centrally is top-sliced for central services, and the remainder is allocated to departments or faculties which operate as semi-autonomous budget centres.
4 Income is received at the centre but most of it is passed on to departments or faculties which 'buy' services from central service units.
5 Earmarked grants are top-sliced at the centre and then allocated according to the contractual arrangements under which they were provided.
6 Income earned by the operating units for the provision of specific services is retained at the centre which administers it on behalf of departments according to detailed institution-wide regulations.
7 Income earned by the operating units is subjected to a levy to cover central costs and the remainder is retained by the budget centres which earned it.
8 All income earned by operating units is retained and all central administration and services are 'bought' as they are needed.

One could regard each of these as a step along a path where some institutions may wish to proceed to the end but others may be happier stopping half way. The point at which any institution stops will depend upon its managerial culture and style and its size, but the monitoring process and information system will need to be able to reflect properly the structure of the resource allocation process. A resource allocation and delegation model which follows the most complex of the scenarios outlined above cannot work if the monitoring system is capable of handling no more than a simple cost centre scheme.

A possible solution for institutions planning to devolve is to adopt a phased approach to charging for overheads which adopts a principle of transparency. In the early stages of a scheme, overheads may be top-sliced but analysed and holders of delegated budgets should be made aware of the costs. This can then move on to a debate on appropriate charging mechanisms with illustrative examples of the alternative approaches before a final move is made to full recharging. The management information may then be adapted gradually to suit the changing needs. However, in practical terms it is advisable to keep the exercise simple and to use as few cost drivers as possible, within the obvious requirement to produce reasonable accuracy. Given the inevitably arbitrary nature of some elements in even the most sophisticated of costing systems, one could argue that absolute accuracy is, in any event, unachievable.

Treatment of capital expenditure

Capital expenditure may be defined as expenditure on items which benefit the organization over more than one accounting period, typically expenditure on land, buildings, plant and machinery, described as fixed assets. The expenditure is recorded in the balance sheet and each year a depreciation charge is levied on the income and expenditure account to reflect the diminution in the value of the item over its useful life. To avoid causing unnecessary complexity by recording minor items, institutions will normally set a minimum value on items to be treated as capital expenditure. Capitalization values will vary between institutions, some may capitalize items with a value in excess of £5000, others perhaps at £10,000, there is no nationally agreed standard. However, the level should be consistent within an institution.

The accounting treatment of capital expenditure can lead to confusion within delegation schemes if budget-holders do not understand the difference between the 'cash' position and the accounting position. Figure 7.3 illustrates the point.

Whilst Figure 7.3 simplifies the position, it illustrates the problem. In terms of management of the budget of the institution, nothing has changed. However, accounting practice has produced a 'better' result. This can lead to problems within institutions which produce detailed management accounts if budget centre managers fail to understand the situation and assume the retained surplus can be spent. Monitoring information needs to clarify this point.

Dissemination of information: paper or online?

Most schemes will produce reports to budget-holders on paper. Whilst this is fairly expensive in terms of use of paper and staff time taken to produce and distribute reports, senior management can at least be satisfied that the information has been received by managers,

1 'Cash' approach

	£
Funds allocated to budget centre	1,000,000
Total expenditure (adjusted for accruals and prepayments)	975,000
Underspend (surplus) carried forward	
and added to next year's allocation	**£25,000**

However, within the expenditure figure above, there may be items which, under the financial accounting rules, are classified as acquisition of fixed assets. Say, in this case, £80,000.

2 Financial accounting approach

	£	£
Total allocation		1,000,000
Total expenditure (as above)	975,000	
Less Purchase of fixed assets	(80,000)	895,000
Depreciation of fixed assets		8,000
Retained surplus		**£97,000**

Figure 7.3 Illustration of the effect of accounting practice on apparent surpluses

especially if they are required to sign as confirmation of receipt. Ensuring that managers read and act on the information is less simple but a requirement to provide explanations for budget variances above a certain percentage is an effective means of ensuring that budget-holders regularly review their expenditure.

An alternative approach is to provide budget-holders with online enquiry facilities to enable them to interrogate their own data within the accounting system. This is expensive in terms of initial set-up costs and will require security controls to prevent staff accessing data outside their field of responsibility. However, once set up it is easier to operate as there is no need for the finance office to go through the laborious process of producing and distributing reports. It also allows budget-holders to obtain up-to-date information whenever they need it rather than having to wait until month-end reports are produced. Combined with the discipline of variance reporting described above, such an approach has considerable advantages.

Departmental 'profit and loss accounts'

Resource allocation to departments, regardless of whether or not delegation is practised, does not necessarily follow the pattern of income earned. The funding councils, for example, 'do not require institutions to replicate the Council's approach to establishing allocations for teaching when making their own internal allocations' (HEFCW 2000). Cross-subsidy then arises where some budget centres within an institution are resourced at a level above that of the income they attract, that additional resourcing being funded by other budget centres which are, thus, resourced at a level below the income they attract. In accounting terms, some clearly generate surpluses and some deficits. Cross-subsidy is widespread throughout higher education. The National Audit Office (1994) found that over half the sector had identified cross-subsidy, with the remainder not having systems in place capable of doing so. In addition, for example, 'St Edmund's Hall, Oxford's third poorest college, is about to win a major share of the Central College Contribution Fund for cross-subsidising poorer colleges' (Baty 1998: 3). Production of monitoring information in a scheme of delegation, in the form of profit and loss accounts, may focus attention on this fact and may increase pressure from the 'losers' to move the institution towards a situation where the internal distribution of funds matches the inflow of grant and fees to the institution. There are strategic issues here which need to be addressed in order to avoid internal frustrations. Tomkins and Mawditt (1994: 28) state that: 'a university may decide that it wishes to offer enhanced teaching in a subject which costs more than that implied by the guide price set by HEFCE. There is nothing inherently wrong with such a decision'. This decision needs to be part of a clearly defined policy and budget-holders need to understand from the start of the scheme that this is the case; participation in the setting-up of the scheme and in the development of the monitoring and information flow is, again, the key.

Policies regarding accumulation and application of departmental reserves

The expectation of budget-holders in a scheme of delegation may, quite justifiably, be that they should be allowed to retain all underspends or 'profits'. Consideration needs to be given to whether this is the best option for budget-holders and senior management. Common sense suggests that a delegated financial management scheme will be of limited success if budget-holders are not permitted to build up reserves. Clawing back underspends to the centre simply encourages the tendency to squander money at year-end rather than lose it. However, allowing budget-holders to retain all surpluses may act as an incentive for senior management to delegate less in order to accumulate central reserves. Much of the 'slack' which exists in budgets which are controlled centrally may be lost in schemes of delegation. For example, staff turnover tends to produce savings which boost the year-end surplus in a centralized scheme but this benefit may be lost if delegated budget-holders are in a position to divert those savings. Some compromise position may be desirable in order to maximize the benefits of the scheme.

One option worthy of consideration is a system of 'taxing' delegated budget surpluses and clawing back an element into central reserves. Thus budget-holders could, perhaps, be allowed to retain 50 per cent and 50 per cent would be clawed back. The question is, what level of 'tax' would be viable (if, indeed, a viable level exists)? It is unlikely that a level of more than 20 per cent would be tolerated; higher than that is likely to prompt a return to the problem of 'spend rather than lose'. A 'taxation' system is also likely to lead to requests for past deficits to be written off against current surpluses for purposes of calculating the clawback to central reserves, and this would be difficult to administer.

The question of deficits needs to be addressed early on when devising a scheme. Budget-holders cannot be given unlimited freedom to anticipate future years' allocations, and a limit on deficits must be set. Given the potential effect of all departments deciding to overspend in one year, that level needs to be fairly low: 10 per cent or 15 per cent would seem to be the acceptable limit where a scheme continues to hold staffing cost control centrally. Where staffing budgets are also delegated, the percentage will need to be lower still, as any deficit arising as a result of an overspend on the staff budget may recur for several years if the cause is an excess of permanent posts.

Again, there is a danger of developing overcomplex systems, and, whilst it is important to consider issues such as these, it must continue to be borne in mind that the system should be managed within constrained administrative resources. The scheme of delegation should be designed to enhance the efficiency of the prime function of the organization, which is providing higher education, not running administrative systems.

One question which may arise is to do with the treatment of interest earned on reserves. Should departmental budgets be credited with interest or should all interest receipts be treated as central funds? In the final analysis, loss of interest to the central budget will only result in a tendency to delegate less or to claw back more of the surplus at the year-end. The complication of interest payment may be one which is best left out, at least in the early years of a scheme.

When considering the policy regarding reserves one must, ultimately, recognize that if serious problems arise owing, for example, to a rapid decline in student numbers or a severe cutback in funding council grant, the senior management of the institution must retain ownership of all reserves and retain the right to claw back delegated reserves. This power should be used only in cases of severe difficulty and as a measure of last resort, and budget-holders should not be left with the impression that reserves may be clawed back on a whim. It would, however, be unacceptable for extensive and painful cuts to be actioned in one area of an institution's work, owing to short-term financial problems, when other departments were holding substantial reserves. The financial, academic and quality arguments will need to be weighed very carefully, however, before a final decision is taken to claw back delegated funds.

Whatever the policy decided on, it needs to be clearly stated as simply as possible in the rules of the scheme of delegation. As an example, Staffordshire University states:

> Currently, departments are not allowed to spend over £10,000 from balances accumulated from previous years without reference to the executive. Interest on balances is not allocated to schools . . . Underspends on school budgets are carried forward to the school's balance. The value of overspends are clawed back in the following year.
>
> (CIPFA 1997: 64)

Staff involved in monitoring schemes need to be kept fully informed of departmental intentions regarding reserves in order that they understand the implications of potential overspends.

Debt collection and policies regarding provision for bad debts

All institutions suffer some level of bad debt and it is likely that, as students are required to pay more out of their own or their parents' pockets, this level will deepen. Debt collection is usually a responsibility of the finance office, but in a scheme of delegation of both expenditure and income (a profit centre scheme) the question of where to charge bad debts needs to be considered. The simplest approach is to treat the provision for bad debts as a central budget item which is top-sliced before funds are allocated to departments. The misery is shared equally. However, as student retention becomes more important in terms of an institutional performance indicator there may be a case for charging bad debts to the department where the student studied, especially if it is the case that the majority of bad debts are due to students dropping out of courses and not paying all or part of the tuition fee due. If such a decision is taken then monitoring procedures will need to provide sufficient analysis of debt for departmental managers to be able to estimate the likely impact on their budgets.

Management (avoidance) of VAT and corporation tax

Higher education institutions in the UK have charitable status for tax purposes and, generally speaking, cannot recover value added tax (VAT) on expenditure but are not liable for corporation tax on any surpluses they generate. This is a complex area best left to the experts, but budget centre managers should be aware that proper management of the institution's tax affairs can lead to savings. It is possible in certain circumstances to recover VAT on a limited range of purchases. The large firms of tax consultants are adept at developing schemes which exploit loopholes in the system. However, Her Majesty's Customs and Excise is equally adept at closing the loopholes at short notice.

From a monitoring point of view, it is important for the central administration to be aware of any effective tax management schemes which may be available and to make sure that sufficient information is available from budget centres to ensure that VAT is both properly charged on outputs and recovered, wherever legally possible, on inputs.

Corporation tax does not become an issue unless a department becomes involved in commercial activity to such an extent that the Inland Revenue has cause to question its charitable status. Proper use of subsidiary companies to channel commercial activities is vital in such circumstances (see chapter 12 in Palfreyman and Warner 1998).

Role of the finance office

In the final analysis, all the theories, books on good practice, research and government exhortations that exist in respect of devolution will be of no use if there are not enough staff to carry out the monitoring function. No one will thank a senior management team which introduces a scheme of devolution which fails owing to inadequate resourcing of the control and monitoring aspects. A scheme of delegation needs a good financial management information system and good quality, experienced staff who can command the trust and respect of departments. The role of an effective finance office should be to monitor, control, facilitate and support a scheme of delegation in such a way that the governing body and senior management team have confidence in the monitoring and control functions and budget-holders have confidence in the facilitation and support they receive. A difficult task.

There are two main ways of operating: either by retaining a centralized finance function or by devolving the function to departments. Both have their advantages and disadvantages.

Centralized approach

The centralized approach has the advantage of maintaining a corporate view; in addition, economies of scale make it easier and cheaper to appoint well-qualified and experienced staff who can work on standardized effective systems. The key disadvantages are remoteness from the point of delivery, which results in lack of detailed knowledge of individual departments' needs, and the risk of developing an 'us and them' culture. Much of the content of this chapter will seem obvious to staff in finance offices who have direct experience of monitoring requirements. However, the finance function may be accustomed to a policing rather than a facilitating role. This could be damaging in a scheme of delegation, and if a centralized approach is adopted then the culture and attitudes of the finance office need to be carefully considered and, if necessary, moves made to ensure that finance staff recognize the need to act as facilitators as well as controllers. Parallels may be drawn with the introduction of local management of schools in the primary and secondary sectors in the UK, where many local education authorities appointed finance staff to posts specifically designed to promote a helpful flow of information both from and to the centre. Finance managers, when they embark upon the development of monitoring schemes, should contemplate that, 'A university cannot be run without consensus and co-operation. It may have a terribly efficient management structure, have a financial control system of impeccable accuracy and be able to cost and account for every item of expenditure, but if in the process of gaining this managerial world the soul of the institution is lost, where is the profit?' (Warwick 1985).

Devolved approach

The advantages and disadvantages of the devolved approach tend to be the opposite of the above. Closeness to the point of delivery gives greater understanding of the local needs and the perception that the departmental finance officer is part of the team may lead to greater openness. However, the finance function may become remote from the centre with a resultant tendency for finance staff to 'go native' and neglect their responsibility to monitor strategic issues. The cost of professionally qualified staff is high, and departments may be resistant to paying for them within tightly constrained budgets. There is also a risk that finance staff in departments will set up their own systems and come to rely on those more than on the centralized accounting package.

On balance, the best approach may be to delegate routine functions such as order processing, payment of invoices and debt recovery whilst maintaining a well qualified professional central service responsible for managing the financial information systems and carrying out the monitoring function. Overall, a centralized approach is likely to be the more cost effective but, returning to the issue of charging for central services, one should remember to split the cost of the finance function between the costs of servicing the departments and the costs of servicing the strategic monitoring needs of senior management and the governing body.

Conclusion

It may be seen that the monitoring role is complex if all stakeholders are to be satisfied. The challenge is to develop an integrated financial reporting system which produces data to suit the needs of all. However, in reality, there is little choice as the level of powerful external influence over the nominally autonomous UK higher education institutions is now so high that all will soon need to produce extensive monitoring information regardless of the extent of delegation which they have. The Transparency Review and the Costing and Pricing Initiative will, alone, enforce a need to produce financial monitoring information at the lowest level of organizational structures.

There may be some reluctance to move in this direction but, in a system where growth in student numbers can be achieved only within a tightly constrained total funding envelope, it is incumbent upon institutions to examine critically their costs in order to improve efficiency. Also, self-examination acts as protection against external intervention. Institutions which decide on resource allocation on the basis of sound strategic principles and compare expenditure with income will be able to justify any cross-subsidy which may exist. Sector-wide failure to do this may provoke changes to grant methodologies which lead to a more directed allocation of funds, with specific grants to subject areas becoming the norm. The Committee of Public Accounts has sounded the warning by stating, with regard to Southampton Institute, that, 'we are astonished that a body with an annual turnover exceeding £49 million a year, and with public funding of £34.2 million in 1996/97, does not have the internal costing systems necessary to manage their operations properly and ensure the appropriate use of public money' (Committee of Public Accounts 1999: para. 4(iv)). It is possible, however, that, in fact, Southampton Institute's systems were a typical example of what existed in higher education institutions before the recent costing initiatives.

▪ 8

DEPARTMENTAL PERSPECTIVE ▪

Jointly authored with
Peter Hodson

Introduction ▪

So far we have been concerned with the process of managing financial resources primarily from a top-down institutional perspective. As a balance to this earlier approach, this chapter gives a departmental perspective (see also Bolton 2000). In many respects, however, the management of financial resources at a departmental level follows the same principles as apply at an institutional level. Thus, there will be a need:

- to understand the way in which income is attracted to the department;
- to formulate long-term strategic plans and to convert these into shorter-term operational plans;
- to devise an equitable, transparent and incentives-driven system of resource allocation to groups and individuals within the department;
- to create a budget based on projected income against operational plans;
- to monitor expenditure against budget; and
- to evaluate achievement against strategic objectives.

We do not repeat here the material in earlier chapters, but rather focus on issues specific to the management of resources at a departmental level. We therefore begin with a few contextual comments and then review the role of heads of department and staffing issues.

Context ∎

Throughout earlier chapters a common theme has been that, as government expenditure per student on higher education has decreased in real terms and institutions have had to look for alternative sources of income, the process of financial management has spread to an ever-widening section of the institution.

This movement has been evident in the UK since the early 1980s. The government cuts of 1981 and continuing decline in the unit of resource (see Chapter 2) have brought about a significant shift in attitude and approach at a departmental level. Staff have seen their day-to-day activities directly influenced by financial decisions being taken by their institution in response to the external environment. The introduction of devolved, formula-based systems of resource allocation, with transparent income and expenditure accounts for each department or cost centre, narrowed the spotlight and put pressure on those members of staff in departments where expenditure was greater than income. In particular, the abolition of tenure in the pre-1992 universities brought a degree of insecurity not previously experienced in that part of the sector. Staff became increasingly aware of the relationship between their individual activities, the income generated by those activities and the financial health of their department. Jobs could become insecure if the department could not generate sufficient income to sustain current staffing levels. Consequently, for many members of staff, there became an element of self-interest in seeking to raise income.

These financial pressures have been accompanied by increased demands for accountability and external assessment which have themselves added to the workload of academic staff. The research assessment exercise (RAE), begun in 1986, added a competitive element to the allocation of research funds, whilst the early 1990s saw the introduction of teaching quality assessments and audits of institutions' quality procedures (see Chapter 2).

It is not only in the UK where these pressures have been felt. In countries and institutions where a centralist approach to financial management has been maintained, it may still be the case that a junior or, indeed even, a more senior academic member of staff may have little appreciation of the financial policies of their institution and even less opportunity to influence those policies. There is a tendency in many parts of the world, however, to reform systems of financial management in such a way as to introduce approaches that widen responsibility for, and awareness of, the financial health of the institution. Often this has been accompanied by economic policies that have involved reduction in government grants which frequently translate into worsening staff/ student ratios.

As a consequence of these additional pressures and workloads arising from higher staff/student ratios, lack of time has become as critical as lack of financial resources. There is simply not enough time for academics to undertake all the teaching, research, community activities, income-generation and administrative chores that are demanded of them without prioritizing activities and focusing on how each individual can best contribute to the department as a whole. Consequently, academic activities have become more managed. That has implications both for those who are now expected to undertake management functions and for those being managed. In particular, it highlights two schools of thought on the management of institutions:

• The first maintains that it is the responsibility of institutional managers to protect academics from the harshness of the external environment and to allow them as much time as possible to concentrate on academic matters free from financial and other administrative responsibilities that might divert them from their primary academic tasks.
• The second maintains that financial pressures are not the sole concern of administrators at the centre of the institution and that in order to compensate for decreasing government support via income-generation and cost-saving measures, the reality of the external environment needs to be recognized and felt throughout the institution.

These two approaches reflect the debate about the extent to which devolution of responsibility is necessary if the institution is to achieve its academic goals. As we have seen in earlier chapters, approaches are likely to vary according to a range of local factors at both an institutional and departmental level. Consequently, there will be no single departmental perspective. Departments vary according to discipline, size and culture. Staff vary according to age, experience and seniority. What is clear, however, is that the ever-increasing pressures of time and financial constraint have a particular impact at a departmental level, because this is the point of delivery of the core business within the institution.

Role of heads of department

Ask any head of department to list their major concerns and high on the list will be something along the lines of, 'there aren't enough financial resources'. This response is as familiar in overseas countries as it is in the UK, although the scale of the problem will differ. Serious as the problems of underfunding have become in the UK, they do not compare with problems of non-payment of salaries, insufficient paper to circulate agenda for meetings and non-existent funds for equipment which are features of the financial situation and resulting management problems in some other countries. In all countries, too, this response reflects only half the problem: there are issues about insufficient resources, but there are also issues about how to make the most efficient and effective use of resources that are available. These two issues are both of concern to heads of department.

Multidimensional approach

In addressing these issues a head of department has to adopt a multi-dimensional approach, the complex nature of which may sometimes lead to tensions, if not conflicts of interest. It is here suggested that heads have to look in three directions at once:

1 *Upwards to the institution.* It is here that heads of department will have to represent the interests of their department. Staff who are sufficiently senior to hold such posts are also likely to be called upon to sit on a range of committees involved in the management of the institution. This will place them in a good position to interact with other senior members of staff and to understand and influence the strategic direction of the institution. In the context of the current discussion, it is imperative that heads of department understand both the basis of financial allocations to departments and the strategic planning process so as to gain maximum benefit for their department. They will need to balance their departmental representational role with their more corporate institutional, managerial role.

2 *Outwards to the external environment.* Again this is a representational role that can bring significant advantages to the department. A head of department who is well networked at a national and professional level can access information that can stand the department in good stead in seeking outside funds. Moreover, senior members of institutions are called upon to play many roles. Peer review is an established aspect of the academic scene in the UK, which means that a head of department could one day be preparing material for assessment whilst another day be sitting in judgement on submissions from another institution. Experience

in playing an assessment role can provide valuable insights for the benefit of their department when it comes to submitting for research council funding, the RAE or future Quality Assurance Agency (QAA) subject reviews.

3 *Inwards to their department.* To some extent the range of representational roles mentioned above has always been present for senior members of staff, although with the increasing imperative to attract non-government funds, an additional pressure is present. Arguably, however, it is in the management of the department that the responsibilities have become significantly more arduous. In this capacity, heads of department are acting as middle managers and as such suffer from all the well-known pressures of that position. They are constantly inundated with demands from the institution's higher management both in terms of more efficient and effective departmental performance as judged by academic criteria or performance indicators in the form of research and teaching assessments and financial performance in terms of income-generating activity and cost savings. These pressures have to be passed down to staff in the department who themselves react with pleas relating to lack of resources and lack of time. At this level the integration of financial, personnel and space considerations becomes a reality, together with such issues as health and safety. Winning a research grant or an industrial contract may be essential for the academic standing and financial health of the department, but, for the head of department, decisions will have to be taken as to where the associated new members of staff will be located and from where any extra desks and equipment will be found. Indeed, it is the whole physical environment that needs to be addressed with its associated risk assessment, health and safety checks and support environment. In the preparation phase there will also have been discussions with the central administration about overhead costs.

Implications

There are some inevitable consequences that arise from the need for heads of department to adopt a more managerialist approach. In particular:

• The appointment of heads of department has to be subject to rigorous procedures. In those institutions in which rotation of senior members of staff as head of department has been traditional, there may need to be a change in historical procedures with the introduction of some form of appointment or monitoring of the process to ensure that a suitable candidate assumes office.

• When senior academic posts are advertised it may be necessary to take into account managerial as well as academic credentials if the person appointed may at some stage be expected to act as head of department.

• Responsibilities as head of department will need to be recognized through additional remuneration. These responsibilities may differ depending upon the size of department and as a consequence some form of sliding scale of payment may need to be introduced.

• Training and staff development in preparation for headship of department needs to be in place. Some aspects may be undertaken within the institution, but there may also be benefit in establishing regional or national schemes to enable heads and potential heads of department to exchange views and experiences and to discuss concerns away from their immediate environment.

Academic staffing issues

Whilst more junior members of the academic staff may not have the managerial responsibilities of their senior colleagues, they cannot help being affected by a financial environment that lays constraints on institutional support for their work, their personal salaries and support for students. The impact of these issues creates the environment in which time becomes a precious commodity.

In the UK, as in many countries, there is a debate about the balance between institutional autonomy and public accountability. The current focus on enhanced accountability, which finds expression in, for instance, quality assessments of teaching and the RAE, has increased pressure on staff not only to perform well in their teaching and research but also to undertake all the preparatory administrative work involved in such assessments. These pressures are in addition to demands to make research grant applications, create links with industry and the local community, and to develop curricula and programmes that will meet the needs and expectations of an increasingly demanding student clientele whilst also attending to their pastoral care.

There was a time when academics were expected to spread their time between teaching and research duties, to take their fair share of departmental administrative chores and to take their turn as a member of a range of departmental and institutional committees. To ensure comparability between members of staff, some heads of department developed a 'brownie points' system with various activities attracting certain credits. Each member of the department would be expected to conduct activities that attracted roughly the same number of credits, giving a balanced workload for all staff.

In recent years, external pressure has forced heads of department to be even more directive in their approach to staff management with a view to gaining the maximum benefit for the department in external assessments. For example, staff with a flourishing research programme that could lead to publication in high quality journals and thereby earn a high grade in the RAE are likely to be encouraged to pursue their research and to have a lighter teaching load as a consequence. Staff who have a natural entrepreneurial flair and are able to develop links with industry and thereby attract much needed external income will similarly be encouraged to develop these activities.

This means, however, that staff who do not have high flying research programmes or industrial links will be expected to undertake more than the average amount of teaching. There is a danger in all of this. Teaching is likely to be relegated in importance and allocated to staff who are not involved in the more obvious income-generating activities. This has been a natural response to an environment in which funding of research is directly related to quality in a way which does not apply to the funding of teaching (see Chapter 4) and in which non-government income has to be generated to sustain the level of activity and infrastructural support deemed essential.

Despite this inevitable focus on activities that directly influence the level of income generation, a wise head of department will recognize that there are more subtle considerations to take into account. Income from teaching represents a high percentage of a department's income. Staff dedicated to teaching are, therefore, 'earning' significant sums for their department, although the relationship between performance and funding may not be as clearly differentiated as with other staff activities. Moreover, the abolition of the binary line in 1992 has led to more competition amongst institutions. Part of that competition has been for good students. High grades in teaching quality assessments or subject reviews can form an important element in an effective marketing strategy to attract both UK students and students from abroad. In some institutions the fee income from non-EU students is a significant proportion of their income and as a consequence a high quality teaching reputation should be regarded as essential.

In some institutions these choices will be influenced by the terms of staff contracts. In the UK, the contract of staff in the older universities is flexible, with no mention of the number of hours to be worked or the percentage of time to be allocated to each activity. Staff in newer universities or other higher education institutions, however, may have contracts that specify the maximum number of contact hours, with recognition of the preparation time associated with each contact hour. In many of the new universities, with a history which has been highly focused on teaching, these contracts may now be perceived as an absolute in the working conditions of the sector. Hence the contracts can be used to support a degree of conservatism when senior management wishes to encourage a diversification of activities.

The level of detail in contracts of employment can be of particular significance in countries undergoing transition to a market economy. In such cases, institutional reform can often incorporate curriculum change with a shift of emphasis away from high contact time towards greater emphasis on self-learning on the part of students. That requires an ability on the part of the institution to shift resources towards the provision of enhanced library and computer facilities and other learning materials often to be written by members of staff. There is also a need to encourage research applicable to the new economic and social climate of the region or nation. These changes can be difficult to achieve when employment contracts provide for payment according to the number of contact hours undertaken by each member of staff.

This increase in differentiation between staff has implications for promotion criteria:

- If staff are being encouraged to spend time on income-generating activities then their success in that area needs to be recognized in their remuneration and promotion prospects.
- On the other hand, in some institutions, staff who are asked to focus on teaching activities may regard their promotion prospects as being in jeopardy. Traditionally, promotion in the older universities in the UK has been perceived to be heavily influenced by research strength, notwithstanding the traditional wording in promotion criteria that teaching, research and other activities will be taken into account. Consequently, if such factors are not directly addressed then issues of staff morale will arise with feelings of 'second-class citizens'.

It is not only promotion criteria that are affected by current demands. Other forms of incentives also need to be developed to meet the aspirations of individuals and the institution. Responses to the current environment have included the following:

- the development of consultancy arrangements, usually negotiated as part of an institution-wide scheme, whereby a member of staff may retain a percentage of the funds generated from external contracts obtained by that individual; and

- the establishment of departmental funds held against the name of individual members of staff reflecting external contracts generated by that member of staff. He or she may then call upon those funds for, say, extra equipment, attendance at a conference or for teaching or technical assistance. On the basis of substantial external earnings it may be possible, for instance, for a member of staff to 'buy themselves out of teaching' for a period of time so that they may focus on research activity. Accumulated funds would then be used to employ on a short-term basis another member of staff to undertake teaching duties. Such arrangements must be treated with care, however, in view of the need to maintain the quality of teaching provision, but they can create an opportunity of employment for a person aspiring to an academic career.

This last point is indicative of a more general trend towards an increase in the number of staff on temporary contracts. In many respects, short-term appointments are unsatisfactory. Individuals will be concerned with securing a more permanent position whilst the institution will have concerns about continuity, commitment and quality assurance. This development is, however, an inevitable consequence of a higher percentage of a department's income being short term in nature, whether from research grants, contracts or overseas fee income. Such income is essential, but there are dangers in entering into long-term commitments on the basis of funds that may be short term in nature. The conflict between EU employment legislation and the length of continuous employment, which may give rise to permanent employment rights if the contract is not correctly established, is a feature of the current short-term approach.

Strategic considerations ■

The need to ensure that staff are focused on activities that bring maximum advantage to the department impinges not only on the balance of their activities as discussed above but also on the activities that the department can afford to support. Freedom to teach and to research in subjects of a lecturer's choice was long held to be one of the principles that attracted staff to a career in higher education. There have always been practical constraints on this principle, but financial pressures now add to those constraints. Whilst in the humanities there is still the opportunity for lone researchers to conduct individual scholarship, the approach in many science-based departments is to focus on a limited number of key areas of activity so that maximum use can be made of equipment, space and financial resources. In teaching, the greater the level of detail required by the Quality Assurance Agency in the programme specification used for course approval, the less freedom exists for individual teachers, because much more of the learning process and the learning outcomes is defined.

For heads of department this means establishing a clear strategy for the department and ensuring that staff appointments are consistent with that strategy. There is also a requirement to ensure that teams are coherent and have leaders that can bring the best out of their colleagues. For more junior members of staff there is a requirement to adapt their interests to the main thrust of their department.

In developing this departmental strategy the same principles apply as were discussed in earlier chapters when considering the development of institutional strategy. In particular, there will need to be:

• integration of academic aspirations with a realistic assessment of available funding, the skills and interests of staff, and available space and equipment; and
• ownership of the department's aspirations and strategic direction by the department as a whole. This implies good communication and a decision-making process that involves staff at all levels.

Institutions vary in the amount of top-down direction and bottom-up initiative in the planning process. In earlier chapters we have urged an integrated approach in which there is an iterative process leading to the formulation of institutional goals whilst encouraging departmental flexibility to develop initiatives that are consistent with those goals. In reality there will be local factors that will determine the extent of departmental freedom in establishing its strategic direction. In formulating a strategic plan there is advantage in consulting staff from the central administration. This can be of particular benefit in those institutions in which there is a devolved, formula-based system of resource allocation. In these cases, a head of department can create a number of 'what if' scenarios to assess the impact of a range of strategies. For instance, a department may need to know the impact over a period of years of planned retirements of staff or the impact of increasing its number of overseas students.

As for the institution as a whole, these strategic considerations should influence the way in which resources are allocated within the department. Just as there needs to be an incentive for departments that attract income to the institution, so there needs to be an incentive for individuals who contribute to the department. Ultimately however, rewards should follow achievement and not proposals, so a particular responsibility for a head of department will be the monitoring of success against agreed plans. Equally, there must be effective monitoring of expenditure. As discussed in earlier chapters, effective monitoring and the extent of departmental responsibilities will be dependent upon the quality of the institution's management information system. There must be consistency of information used by departmental and institutional managers. Lack of confidence in the institution's system can often lead to the establishment of local systems within a department. These may be designed to satisfy the needs of departmental managers, but there arise issues of reconciliation with data from other systems which can be time consuming and can lead to a lack of consistency and loss of data integrity. As a result, incorrect analysis and decision making in the operational activity will occur and poor management control of expenditure may result.

Conclusion ■

The picture that emerges, whether from the UK or elsewhere, is that external pressure has made the management of departments more complex and far more authoritative and interventionist in character. Although we are here concerned with issues of financial management, those issues impinge on a wide range of responsibilities held by those in a senior departmental position. They may be summarized as including the following:

- representing the department in the institution's decision-making forums, in particular in ensuring that any revision in resource allocation methodology is fair (some might say advantageous) to the department;
- understanding thoroughly the basis on which the institution and the department attract income;
- understanding thoroughly the various coefficients in the institution's resource allocation model, how they influence the department's annual allocation and how the department can utilize the prevailing methodology to its best advantage;
- being instrumental in the formulation of a departmental strategic plan and ensuring that financial, staff and space resources are allocated to the achievement of the plan;
- ensuring that staff are focused on the importance of income-generating activities and that systems of support are established

within the department to assist staff to identify and take advantage of opportunities that exist;

- establishing and monitoring quality assurance and enhancement procedures in the department with a view to benefiting financially from any schemes that link funding to quality;
- drawing up an annual budget that is focused on achieving the department's strategic objectives;
- establishing transparent mechanisms for the allocation of funds within the department;
- ensuring that departmental resources are efficiently and effectively used and that there is a system in place to monitor expenditure;
- providing academic and managerial leadership and motivating staff in the interests of themselves and the department, recognizing that staff are most effective when there is consistency between their interests and the interests of the institution;
- ensuring that the contribution of members of staff to income generation is appropriately recognized in personal remuneration and promotion procedures;
- finding a balance between academic and managerial activities to maintain strong academic leadership in the department;
- maintaining external links and raising the profile of the department with external agencies;
- ensuring that personnel policies, such as staff appraisal schemes, are followed;
- providing effective communication channels to all stakeholders;
- ensuring that effective curriculum development is undertaken to maintain an attractive portfolio;
- fulfilling any delegated health and safety and risk assessment responsibilities; and
- translating university policy into departmental action.

9

CONSOLIDATION

Introduction

The previous chapters have considered various aspects of the process of financial management. The first three chapters provided an introduction, set the historical context and dipped into the theory underlying aspects of financial management. The next three chapters delved into the principles of resource allocation. Various sources of income were explained and the ways in which that income can be distributed to the various component parts of the institution were explored. The importance of seeing financial management as part of the wider process of institutional planning was stressed. Given current trends in management practice, there was a particular focus on issues relating to devolution of financial responsibility and formulaic approaches to the allocation of resources. This focus on resource allocation was balanced in the next chapter by a reminder that, whatever system is used for resource allocation, there is an obligation to monitor expenditure and to account for the use of public funds. To counter any suggestion that the previous chapters had adopted a centralist viewpoint, the previous chapter gave a departmental perspective.

Although each of these chapters has focused on a particular issue or aspect of the management of financial resources, there have been a number of themes that have run through all of them. The purpose in this concluding chapter is to identify those themes and to make a few comments to consolidate the earlier discussion. The themes that might be identified are discussed under the headings of: institutional culture, concepts of power, staff training and development, management information systems, structural issues, and the management of change. The chapter concludes with a few observations on managerial implications.

Institutional culture ▮

The thrust of previous chapters has been that systems of financial management have been shifting towards market-orientated approaches. It was seen, for instance, that concepts of devolution and formula-based systems were driven by the desire to bring the realities of the external environment to a budget centre level. In this way, the argument runs, staff will be more responsive to demands for income-generating activity. What has developed, therefore, is the concept of the entrepreneurial institution. Institutions of higher education, however, are complex bodies whose behaviour patterns are influenced by a range of sometimes inconsistent cultural norms. In Chapter 3 we identified a number of traditional cultural models, including collegiality, bureaucracy, organized anarchy, political and entrepreneurialism. The presence and strength of each of these cultures will vary between, and indeed within, institutions. The significance of this for the management of financial resources (Thomas 1996) is two-fold:

1 any change in resource allocation methodology is likely to be influenced by the strength and nature of the prevailing culture; and
2 any change in the methodology is likely to have an impact on the existing institutional culture.

This is consistent with the observation in an earlier chapter that systems of financial management may be approached with two intentions. They may be seen:

1 as part of the bureaucratic mechanism of allocating resources amongst the component parts of an institution; or
2 as a way of changing the culture and behaviour patterns of the institution and its staff.

These two approaches may not be mutually exclusive. Whatever the initial motivation for change, however, in practice any significant change in resource allocation methodology will affect both the mechanics of the process and the culture of the institution. Often, the change will be initiated by senior managers who see the need for a new system. The focus at this stage is likely to be on how the process is to be managed. The vast majority of the institution, however, will be interested not in the 'how' but in the 'how much': their focus will be directed towards the extent to which the changes in the system will affect their budgetary allocation.

For institutional managers there are a number of considerations:

- A conscious decision needs to be taken about the formation of budget centres in the light of the prevailing culture and the responsibilities to be exercised by the budget centre. It is often assumed that academic units are the appropriate management units, but these may be too small to exercise significant managerial and financial flexibility.
- On the other hand, the creation of larger managerial units may lack cohesiveness because of established cultural norms. It is of course possible that such restructuring, involving a breakdown of established cultural behaviour patterns, is an intended outcome in order to shift ingrained conservatism within the institution.
- Cultural characteristics of collegiality may influence managerial activity at a departmental level. The ability and enthusiasm of deans and heads of department to focus on managerial issues may differ between disciplines, with the more science-orientated staff being more adept at responding to a formulaic methodology.
- Although devolved, formula-based systems are intended to introduce the bureaucratic concepts of rationality and objectivity into the resource allocation process, micropolitical activity and concepts of power may still be expected to influence the implementation process.
- Devolution to a departmental level may lead to a decline in collegiality and a reinforcement of the organized anarchy characteristics of the institution with activity based on self-interest.
- Whilst entrepreneurial activity can be outward looking and to the benefit of the institution as a whole, it can also be inward looking and create internal competition between departments.
- Devolved, formula-based systems of resource allocation enhance the power of income-generating departments. Such consequences can skew the shape of the institution and lead to the assumption of evaluative criteria based on financial strength rather than academic merit. The power of a strong financial position at a departmental level can generate an a priori case for expansion, notwithstanding possibilities for greater efficiency through interdepartmental collaboration and integration at a faculty or school level.
- Encouragement of entrepreneurial activity increases the need to monitor departmental activities, establish enhanced budgetary procedures and management information systems and to reconcile information at a central and departmental level.

Concepts of power ▉

One of the particular features of the above discussion has been that relating to micropolitical activity within institutions. Given the rhetoric of rationality that has accompanied recent trends in resource allocation methodology, it might be expected that behaviour patterns associated with sub-unit power would have been affected. Indeed, we saw in the earlier discussion that the rationale for the introduction of such systems has been to break down the influence of powerful individuals and groups. Institutional managers need to be aware, however, that micropolitical power remains a strong force in determining the allocation of resources. In particular:

• Basic decisions continue to be shaped by a dominant group of top management. Initiation of change is likely to be top-down, with detailed work, including the preparation of policy papers, continuing to be undertaken by senior administrators reporting to the vice-chancellor or chief executive.
• Powerful individuals continue to influence resource allocation decisions. Whilst the moves towards formulaic approaches lead to a more mechanistic process once the system has been established, the holders of influential positions at the time that details of the model are being discussed can influence the outcome.
• Although the rationale for change is often seen by senior managers in terms of clarity and fairness in the process, the majority of staff will be concerned primarily with the outcome of the changes in so far as they affect their own departmental and individual interest. The debate on policy proposals is likely to become polarized between those departments benefiting from the change and those losing. Managers and administrators involved in devising the new system should expect the losing departments to adopt tactics that question the validity of the calculations and methodology employed.
• Power accrues to those departments that attract valued resources. The rationale of recent trends in resource allocation has been the encouragement of income generation. That implies incentive schemes that allocate funds to those budget centres that earn those funds. It must be expected, therefore, that the debate will polarize between staff from departments that earn income and who see that income as 'rightfully theirs', and staff from departments where income-generating potential is not so readily available and who believe in some form of equitable distribution according to need.
• Departments that are central to an institution's activities have a disproportionate influence over the resource allocation process.

For instance, those academic departments that offer their own honours degree programmes are in an advantageous position compared with those departments that offer only subsidiary or supporting courses. The latter group of departments is vulnerable to curriculum change that might restrict the number of students attending subsidiary courses.

It is evident from the above that sub-unit power remains a significant factor in the resource allocation process. Rather than eradicating the influence of sub-unit power, the implementation of a devolved formula-based system can generate micropolitical activity based on self-interest and can create new, powerful forces that gain their authority not from perceived closeness to the vice-chancellor or chief executive, but through financial strength as reflected in the resource allocation model. Power resides in those with an ability to understand and manipulate the coefficients in the institutional model.

Staff training and development

Changes in the way in which financial resources are managed will inevitably have an impact on members of staff involved in the process. Indeed, the primary purpose of devolution of financial responsibility may be to affect institutional and individual behaviour patterns. There are several areas in which change in financial management practices will have implications for staffing issues.

- Appointment criteria need to take account of the fact that headship of a department carries significant managerial responsibilities. Academic achievement may have to be balanced with managerial experience and expertise when making senior academic appointments.
- If academic staff are expected to be entrepreneurial and to attract funds to the institution, those who are successful need to be rewarded through the promotions and discretionary payments procedures. Traditional criteria of teaching, research and administrative duties need to be supplemented to reflect current demands on staff.
- If heads of department and deans are to be expected to carry additional financial and managerial responsibilities then they need to be encouraged to attend training programmes. Such programmes can provide not only information on, for instance, budgetary matters and personnel issues, but also an opportunity for participants to share their problems and concerns with others in a similar position, away from the daily pressures that occupy the time of busy staff.

- Just as devolution of financial responsibility brings a training and staff development requirement for academic staff, so too does it bring a requirement to focus on the approach to be adopted by central administrators. Devolution brings with it a need for support and interaction between academic and administrative staff. It could well be argued that effective organizations have always ensured a good relationship between different categories of staff, but devolution brings the issue to the fore. There is an imperative, for instance, for staff in finance offices to explain and provide financial data in a form that is easily understood by the non-specialist. Similarly, the focus of staff in personnel offices is away from a routine establishments function towards the provision of an interactive support function. As Lawler and Galbraith (1993: 71) have suggested: 'staff units need to move away from a control orientation to one of strategic support and expert service'.
- The need for support mentioned above has implications for the structure of institutions. Consideration will need to be given to the extent to which administrative activities should be dispersed and decentralized to the level of the academic activity that they support. Much will depend, however, upon the size and location of the academic unit, for physical decentralization may not be cost effective if devolution is to be to a departmental level.

Management information systems

Trends towards devolved, formula-based systems of resource allocation are dependent for their acceptance on consistent, reliable, timely and easily understood management information. Failure to provide such information will lead to duplication of effort, frustration and a lack of confidence in the scheme. This consistency in the handling of data needs to be across different administrative task areas and between the central administration and academic departments. Moreover, the implementation of enhanced devolution does not absolve the central administration from their monitoring responsibilities. Consequently, sound budgetary procedures need to be in place with regular monitoring and reporting mechanisms. Failure to address such issues can lead to:

- a mismatch between principle and practice in detailed implementation;
- an inability to update information, creating inconsistency in planning data;
- failure to recognize early signs of potential difficulty; and
- the danger of a serious and unexpected financial deficit.

Consequently, there is a relationship between the extent of a devolved, formula-based approach to resource allocation and the need for integrated management information systems. For senior managers there will be a need to consider whether their management information systems are capable of meeting the requirements imposed by a new procedure. The implementation of new systems, however, requires political as well as rational argument. Senior managers will, therefore, need to gain institutional support for investment in any improvements in management information systems that are deemed necessary.

Structural issues ■

Recent trends have affected aspects of institutional structure, in particular issues relating to committee membership, administrative support and the role of deans. For instance:

- The composition of critical committees will influence behaviour patterns, the details of the approach adopted and the level of effectiveness. In particular, the membership of deans or heads of department on resource allocation committees may introduce a conflict between their managerial and representational roles. On the other hand, a smaller committee with a narrower membership base may not be conducive to wide ownership of issues.
- When a budget centre is created above the level of the historically accepted basic unit, there may be pressure to introduce a secondary mechanism for the distribution of resources to those units.
- In order to facilitate effective management at faculty and departmental levels, the introduction of devolved, formula-based systems requires a reorientation of administrative support. This implies a level of decentralization. (For further comments, see above under the section on staff training and development.)

Management of change ■

For those involved in the implementation of change in resource allocation and financial management practices there has to be an appreciation of the complexity of the undertaking, not simply in technical terms but more fundamentally, in behavioural patterns and cultural norms. Studies (Thomas 1995) indicate that:

- institutional models operate as much on micropolitical as on rational patterns of behaviour or values;

* intended actions lead to unintended consequences which have not been foreseen;
* macro-institution-wide issues of implementation are reflected at the micro-level of faculty management;
* the complexity of the change process is more easily explained through understanding cultural interpretations of institutional operations than through a study solely of administrative practices or procedures;
* the leadership styles of major actors are individually and collectively significant for the planning and decision-making processes at the strategic as well as the operational level;
* the lack of a developed technical capability to handle management information directly affects the operation of such models at both its strategic and operational levels; and
* the speed of implementation can affect the institution's ability to prepare its staff to cope with the new methodology.

As a consequence, a multiplicity of strategies for change needs to be employed. Given the complex environment of educational institutions, the change will need to be seen as a sequence of events evolving through different phases. The different elements of the change process may be summarized as follows.

* The presence of a change agent is clearly pivotal. At an institutional level, the appointment of a new vice-chancellor or chief executive is often a significant catalyst for change. For speedy and effective implementation of change, the holder of this post needs to drive the process and be seen to be so doing. Similarly, at the level of a budget centre there needs to be clear leadership. There is a danger, however, that because of the different bases of their appointment, the position of the head of a budget centre might be considerably weaker than that of the vice-chancellor or chief executive at the institutional level. It is important to ensure that authority matches responsibility.
* The background, preferences and leadership style of the change agent will have a significant impact. This person will need to be sensitive to important practical issues as well as to the principles if new systems are to be successfully implemented. Moreover, the degree of grass-roots support for change can be influenced by the change agent's skills in communication. An enthusiastic, open and well-argued approach can engender a positive attitude amongst staff towards the implementation of change. Lack of communication can lead to misunderstandings and an underestimation of the degree of change required.

- Whilst the change process needs to be based on rational, evaluative evidence, it also needs to be supported by political awareness. Reliance on rational approaches is likely to be insufficient. Political awareness and involvement in the decision-making process need to be present. This will involve the change agent in working through established formal mechanisms; in using the power of position as chairman of key committees; activating informal networks to identify and harness the support of those who will benefit from the change; and manoeuvring key actors into positions of support.
- There needs to be an effective bureaucratic phase to convert principles into practice and to ensure the existence and operation of performance monitoring by the central authorities.

Managerial implications ▪

In the light of what has been said above, there are a number of implications for institutional managers involved in the implementation of change in the management of financial resources. They may be summarized as follows.

- The implementation of systems that impinge on the culture of institutions is likely to give rise to a period of hiatus. The introduction of formula-based systems, for instance, can represent a new evaluative methodology that is being used to change the shape of the university. As such it should not be surprising if, in the short term, a destabilizing internal environment is created.
- The change process is likely to affect the tasks of members of staff in terms of income-generating activities, the monitoring of performance and a general emphasis on managerial functions. For the change to be effective, an holistic approach to change should be adopted with an equal focus on strategy, structure, technology and people within changing socioeconomic and technical environments.
- Strong strategic direction is required from the senior management team if a balance is to be maintained between the organized anarchy and collegial elements within an institution.
- There needs to be awareness that the external methodology on which the institution's allocation is based may not itself be 'rational'. To replicate the external system at an internal level may compound such irrationality and fuel micropolitical debate.
- The implementation of formula-based systems of resource allocation can be accompanied by a shift of power away from the central

administration. As external funding bodies have become more transparent in their resource allocation methodology, the raw data that influence internal resource allocation decisions have become more widely available throughout an institution. As a consequence, deans and heads of department are able to undertake their own calculations and use them as a basis for debate.

• Despite the rhetoric of rationality, consistency and transparency which accompanies devolved, formula-based systems, the process of implementation, the determination of coefficients and consequential budgetary allocations and strategic policy remain subject to micropolitical activity, the influence of sub-unit power and the preferences and priorities of key members of staff. Consequently, institutional managers need to be aware that the implementation of such systems is unlikely to diminish the undercurrent of micropolitical activity that has historically accompanied the process of resource allocation. Management remains as much about understanding and harnessing micropolitical activity as about making rational judgements.

• The role of arbiter in terms of the institution's policies and practices is increased to the extent that there needs to be awareness that proposed changes in curricula or teaching arrangements may be motivated by financial rather than by academic considerations.

• A move towards a numerate, analytical and systematic base for decision making can place an increased responsibility on institutional managers for the accuracy of that information in the knowledge that those figures will form the basis of micropolitical activity. Such a system reinforces the influence of officials who are most intimately involved in preparing that information base. Those officials can gain a high profile within the institution.

• The role of facilitation in terms of explaining the details and consequences of the system is increased. Presentation of the system needs to be in terms that are easily understood. Time spent in explaining the consequences of change can be considerable.

• Whilst a formulaic, incentives-driven scheme can encourage an entrepreneurial culture and aid the planning process at a departmental level, it also imposes a bureaucratic responsibility of consistency in methodology. Fundamental changes in the scheme can have a damaging effect on departmental morale.

• There is a danger that a devolved system might increase institutional overhead costs. Such systems are intended to encourage an increase in income streams, but if the cost of operating such schemes outweighs the net increase in income then the goals of the institution will not be enhanced.

- Devolution enhances the need for managerial ability at a budget centre level. This emphasizes the need to appoint key personnel as deans and heads of department and to instigate appropriate training and staff development programmes.
- Heads of budget centres need to be provided with administrative support. This has implications for the structure of the institution's central administration and for the development and training of administrative and managerial staff.

BIBLIOGRAPHY

ABRC (1987) *A Strategy for the Science Base*. London: HMSO.

Allen, M. (1988) *The Goals of Universities*. Milton Keynes: SRHE/Open University Press.

Anderson Report (1960) *Grants to Students: Report of the Committee appointed by the Minister of Education and the Secretary of State for Scotland in June, 1958*, Cmnd 1051. London: HMSO.

Anthony, R.N. (1965) *Planning and Control Systems: A Framework for Analysis*. Boston: Graduate School of Business Administration, Harvard University.

Australian National University (2000) *Finance and Business Manual*. www.anu.edu.au/finance/chart/overview.htm (accessed 16 March 2000).

Balderston, F.E. (1974) *Managing Today's University*. San Francisco: Jossey-Bass.

Baldridge, J.V. (1971) *Power and Conflict in the University*. New York: John Wiley.

Barnes, R.V. (1991) The introduction of budget devolution at the University College of Swansea. Unpublished MSc dissertation, Anglia Polytechnic.

Barnes, W.H.F. (1973) Finance and control of universities: basic principles, in R.E. Bell and A.T. Youngston (eds) *Present and Future in Higher Education*. London: Tavistock.

Batten, C. and Trafford, V.N. (1985) Evaluation: an aid to institutional management, in G. Lockwood and J.L. Davies *Universities: The Management Challenge*, chapter 13. Windsor: SRHE/NFER-Nelson.

Baty, P. (1998) Oxbridge job 'not a hobby', *Times Higher Education Supplement*, 26 June.

Becher, T. (1989) *Academic Tribes and Territories*. Milton Keynes: SRHE/Open University Press.

Becher, T. and Kogan, M. (1992) *Process and Structure in Higher Education*, 2nd edn. London: Routledge.

Beer, S. (1972) *Brain of the Firm*. London: Allen Lane/The Penguin Press.

Berdahl, R.O. (1957) *British Universities and the State*. London: Cambridge University Press.

Bergquist, W. (1993) *The Postmodern Organization.* San Francisco, Jossey-Bass.

Billing, D. and Thomas, H.G. (2000) The international transferability of quality assessment systems for higher education: the Turkish experience, *Quality in Higher Education,* 6(1): 31–40.

Bleau, B.L. (1981) Planning models in higher education: historical review and survey of currently available models, *Higher Education,* 10(2): 153–68.

Bligh, D., Thomas, H.G. and McNay, I. (1999) *Understanding Higher Education.* Exeter: Intellect.

Bolton, A. (2000) *Managing the Academic Unit.* Buckingham: Open University Press.

Booth, C. (1987) Central government and higher education planning 1965–1986, *Higher Education Quarterly,* 41(1): 57–72.

Bosworth, S. (ed.) (1986) *Beyond the Limelight.* Reading: Conference of University Administrators.

Bourn, M. (1993) Caveat emptor: some aspects of cost analysis in universities, *Higher Education Policy,* 6(3): 10–18.

Bourn, M. (1994a) A long and winding road: the evolution of devolution in universities, in R.H. Berry (ed.) *Management Accounting in Universities.* London: Chartered Institute of Management Accountants.

Bourn, M. (1994b) Meeting the indirect costs of support services in universities: top-slicing, charging-out, taxes, trading, and devolution, *Financial Accountability and Management,* 10(4): 323–38.

Bowman, C.C.B. (1990) *The Making of a Corporate Plan.* Unpublished MSc dissertation, Anglia Higher Education College.

Brown, R. (2000) Diversity in higher education: do we really want it? *perspectives: Policy and Practice in Higher Education,* 4(1): 2–6.

Bruton, M.J. (1987) University planning and management in conditions of complexity and uncertainty, *Higher Education Quarterly,* 41(4): 373–89.

Burnett, C., Smith, R. and Silberstein, M. (1994) The first phase in the development of an alternative course costing system, in R.H. Berry (ed.) *Management Accounting in Universities.* London: Chartered Institute of Management Accountants.

Burrell, G. (1993) Eco and the bunnymen, in J. Hassard and M. Parker (eds) *Postmodernism and Organisations,* chapter 4. London: Sage.

Burton, D. (1997) The myth of 'expertness': cultural and pedagogical obstacles to restructuring East European curricula, *British Journal of In-service Education,* 23(2): 219–29.

Cameron, K.S. (1980) Critical questions in assessing organisational effectiveness, *Organisational Dynamics,* 9: 66–80.

Carswell, J. (1985) *Government and the Universities in Britain: Programme and Performance 1960–1980.* Cambridge: Cambridge University Press.

Cave, M., Hanney, S. and Trevett, G. (1988) *The Use of Performance Indicators in Higher Education.* London: Jessica Kingsley.

CIMA (1996) *Devolved Budgeting in the Education Sector.* London: Chartered Institute of Management Accountants.

CIPFA (1996) *A Model Set of Financial Regulations for Further and Higher Education Institutions.* London: Chartered Institute of Public Finance and Accounting.

CIPFA (1997) *Resource Allocation Models in Further and Higher Education: A Compendium.* London: Chartered Institute of Public Finance and Accounting.

CIPFA (1999) *Risk Management.* London: Chartered Institute of Public Finance and Accounting.

Clark, B.R. (1998) *Creating Entrepreneurial Universities: Organizational Pathways of Transformation.* New York: Pergamon.

Clayton, K.M. (1988a) Recent developments in the funding of university research, *Higher Education Quarterly,* 42(1): 20–37.

Clayton, K.M. (1988b) Trends in funding arrangements, *Higher Education Quarterly,* 42(2): 134–43.

Cohen, M.D. and March, J.G. (1974) *Leadership and Ambiguity.* New York: McGraw-Hill.

Committee of Public Accounts (1999) *Overseas Operations, Governance and Management at Southampton Institute.* London: The Stationery Office.

Covaleski, M.A. and Dirsmith, M.W. (1988) An institutional perspective on the rise, social transformation, and fall of a university budget category, *Administrative Science Quarterly,* 33: 562–87.

CUC (1995) *Guide for Members of Governing Bodies of Universities and Colleges in England and Wales.* Bristol: Higher Education Funding Council for England.

Davies, J.L. (1985) The agendas for university management in the next decade, in G. Lockwood and J.L. Davies *Universities: The Management Challenge,* chapter 3. Windsor: SRHE/NFER-Nelson.

Davies, J.L. (1987) *The Entrepreneurial and Adaptive University.* Paris: OECD.

Dearing Report (1997) *Higher Education in the Learning Society.* Report of the National Commission on Higher Education. Norwich: HMSO.

DES (1985) *The Development of Higher Education into the 1990s,* Cmnd 9524. London: HMSO.

DES (1987) *Higher Education – Meeting the Challenge,* Cmnd 114. London: HMSO.

DES (1988) *Education Reform Act.* London: HMSO.

DES (1991) *Higher Education – A New Framework,* Cmnd 1541. London: HMSO.

DES (1992) *Further and Higher Education Act.* London: HMSO.

Devinsky, F. (2000) Running a university in difficult political conditions: the case of Comenius University in Bratislava, *perspectives: Policy and Practice in Higher Education,* 4(3): 80–4.

Donaldson, L. (1987) Strategy and structural adjustment to regain fit and performance: in defence of contingency theory, *Journal of Management Studies,* 24: 1–24.

Dore, R. (1992) Japan's version of managerial capitalism, in T.A. Kochan and M. Useem (eds) *Transforming Organizations,* chapter 2. New York: Oxford University Press.

Drucker, P.F. (1990) *Managing the Non-profit Organization.* London: Butterworth-Heinemann.

Drury, C. (1996) *Management and Cost Accounting,* 4th edn. London: Thomson.

Elkin, J. and Law, D. (2000) *Managing Information.* Buckingham: Open University Press.

Ewart, W. (1985) Managing information, in G. Lockwood and J.L. Davies *Universities: The Management Challenge,* chapter 12. Windsor: SRHE/NFER-Nelson.

Fielden, J. (1982) Strategies for survival, in A. Morris and J. Sizer (eds) *Resources and Higher Education*, chapter 9. Guildford: SRHE.

Fielden, J. (1993) Delegated management and budgets. Unpublished consultancy paper.

Galbraith, J.R. (1993) The value-adding corporation: matching structure with strategy, in J.R. Galbraith, E.E. Lawler III and Associates *Organizing for the Future: The New Logic for Managing Complex Organizations*. San Francisco: Jossey-Bass.

Gaskell, S.M. (1989) Education and culture: a perspective from higher education, *Higher Education Quarterly*, 43(4): 318–31.

Gledhill, J.M. (1999) *Managing Students*. Buckingham: Open University Press.

Groves, R.E.V., Pendlebury, M.W. and Newton, J. (1994) Management accounting information in universities: a Cardiff experiential perspective, in R.H. Berry (ed.) *Management Accounting in Universities*. London: Chartered Institute of Management Accountants.

Hackman, J.D. (1985) Power and centrality in the allocation of resources in colleges and universities, *Administrative Science Quarterly*, 30: 61–77.

Hall, D. and Thomas, H.G. (1999) Higher education reform in a transitional economy: a case study from the School of Economic Studies in Mongolia, *Higher Education*, 38: 441–60.

Handy, C. (1993) *Understanding Organisations*, 4th edn. Harmondsworth: Penguin.

Hanham Report (1988) *Costing and Pricing of University Research and Projects*. London: CVCP.

HEFCE (1994) *Accountability for Research Funds (4/94)*. Bristol: Higher Education Funding Council for England.

HEFCE (1998) *Effective Financial Management and Governance: Recognising the Financial Impact of Decision Making*. Bristol: Higher Education Funding Council for England.

HEFCE (1999) *Funding Higher Education in England*. Bristol: Higher Education Funding Council for England.

HEFCW (1995) *Financial Health Monitoring Procedures*, Circular W95/97HE. Cardiff: Higher Education Funding Council for Wales.

HEFCW (1999) *Audit Code of Practice*. Cardiff: Higher Education Funding Council for Wales.

HEFCW (2000) *Recurrent Grant 2000/2001*, Circular W00/29HE. Cardiff: Higher Education Funding Council for Wales.

Henkel, M. and Little, B. (eds) (1999) *Changing Relationships between Higher Education and the State*. London: Jessica Kingsley.

HEQC (1994) *Higher Education Quality Council Annual Report 1992–93*. London: Higher Education Quality Council.

Hills, F.S. and Mahoney, T.A. (1978) University budgets and organisational decision making, *Administrative Science Quarterly*, 23: 454–65.

Hopwood, A. (1984) Accounting and the pursuit of efficiency, in A. Hopwood and C. Tomkins (eds) *Issues in Public Sector Accounting*. Oxford: Philip Allan.

Hoyle, E. (1982) Micropolitics of educational organisations, *Education Management and Administration*, 10: 87–98.

Humfrey, C. (1999) *Managing International Students*. Buckingham: Open University Press.

ICAEW (1999) *Internal Control: Guidance for Directors on the Combined Code.* London: Institute of Chartered Accountants in England and Wales.

International Federation of Accountants (1998) *Management Accounting Concepts.* International Management Accounting Practice Statement, revised March 1998.

Jarratt Report (1985) *Report of the Steering Committee for Efficiency Studies in Universities.* London: CVCP.

Johnson, H.T. (1994) Relevance regained: total quality management and the role of management accounting, *Critical Perspectives on Accounting,* 5(3): 259–67.

Johnson, H.T. and Kaplan, R.S. (1987) *Relevance Lost: The Rise and Fall of Management Accounting.* Boston: Harvard Business School Press.

Johnston, R.J. (1993) Funding research: an exploration of inter-discipline variations, *Higher Education Quarterly,* 47(4): 357–72.

Joint Funding Councils (1997) *Management Information for Decision Making: Costing Guidelines for Higher Education Institutions.* London: the Higher Education Funding Councils for Wales, England, Scotland and Northern Ireland.

Jonas, S., Katz, R.N., Martinson, L., *et al.* (1997) *Campus Financial Systems for the Future.* Washington, DC: National Association of College and University Business Officers.

Jones, R. and Pendlebury, M. (1996) *Public Sector Accounting,* 4th edn. London: Pitman.

Keeley, M. (1978) A social justice approach to organizational evaluation, *Administrative Science Quarterly,* 23: 272–92.

Keller, G. (1982) *Academic Strategy: The Management Revolution in American Higher Education.* Baltimore: Johns Hopkins University Press.

Kochan, T.A. and Useem, M. (eds) (1992) *Transforming Organizations.* New York: Oxford University Press.

Koder, M. and Hewitt, R. (1992) The application of the Commonwealth Relative Funding Model (1990) within the University of Sydney, *Journal of Tertiary Education,* 14(2): 177–92.

Lawler, E.E. III and Galbraith, J.R. (1993) New roles for the staff function: strategic support and services, in J.R. Galbraith, E.E. Lawler III and Associates *Organizing for the Future: The New Logic for Managing Complex Organizations.* San Francisco: Jossey-Bass.

Leavitt, H.J. (1965) Applied organizational change in industry: structural, technological and humanistic approaches, in J.G. March (ed.) *Handbook of Organizations,* chapter 27. Chicago: Rand-McNally.

Liston, C. (1999) *Managing Quality and Standards.* Buckingham: Open University Press.

Littlewood, M. (1999) Towards the market: managing change in the Czech Republic, *perspectives: Policy and Practice in Higher Education,* 3(1): 23–7.

Lockwood, G. (1985) Planning, in G. Lockwood and J.L. Davies *Universities: The Management Challenge,* chapter 7. Windsor: SRHE/NFER-Nelson.

Lockwood, G. and Davies, J.L. (1985) *Universities: The Management Challenge.* · Windsor, SRHE/NFER-Nelson.

London, N.A. (1996) Decentralisation as and for education reform in Trinidad and Tobago, *Educational Studies,* 22(2): 187–202.

Mauch, J.E. and Sabloff, P.L.W. (eds) (1995) *Reform and Change in Higher Education.* New York: Garland.

McNay, I. (1995a) From the collegial academy to corporate enterprise: the changing cultures of universities, in T. Schuller (ed.) *The Changing University?* Buckingham: SRHE/Open University Press.

McNay, I. (1995b) Universities in a competitive market: a balance sheet, *ETH Bulletin*, June.

Merrison (1982) *Report of a Joint Working Party on the Support of University Scientific Research under the Chairmanship of Sir Alec Merrison*, Cmnd 8567. London: HMSO.

Millett, J.D. (1962) *The Academic Community.* New York: McGraw-Hill.

Mohrman, A.M. Jr and Lawler, E.E. III (1993) Human resource management: building a strategic partnership, in J.R. Galbraith, E.E. Lawler III and Associates *Organizing for the Future: The New Logic for Managing Complex Organizations.* San Francisco: Jossey-Bass.

Moodie, G.C. and Eustace, R. (1974) *Power and Authority in British Universities.* London: George Allen & Unwin.

Moore, P.G. (1987) University financing 1979–86, *Higher Education Quarterly*, 41(1): 25–42.

Morris (1983) *The Support given by Research Councils for In-house and University Research: Report of a Working Party of the ABRC.* London: HMSO.

NAB (1984) *A Strategy for Higher Education in the Late 1980s and Beyond.* London: HMSO.

NAB (1986) *Good Management Practice Studies. Study A: Resource Utilisation and Management Structures*, prepared by Coopers & Lybrand, September.

Nadler, D.A., Gerstein, M.S., Shaw, R.B. and Associates (1992) *Organizational Architecture.* San Francisco: Jossey-Bass.

National Audit Office (1994) *The Financial Health of Higher Education Institutions in England.* London: HMSO.

National Audit Office (1997) *Governance and the Management of Overseas Courses at the Swansea Institute of Higher Education.* London: The Stationery Office.

National Audit Office (1998) *Overseas Operations, Governance and Management at Southampton Institute.* London: The Stationery Office.

National Audit Office (1999a) *Financial Management and Governance at Gwent Tertiary College.* London: The Stationery Office.

National Audit Office (1999b) *Investigation of Alleged Irregularities at Halton College.* London: The Stationery Office.

Newton, R. (1992) The two cultures of academe: an overlooked planning hurdle, *Planning for Higher Education*, 21: 8–14.

Owen, T. (1980) The University Grants Committee, *Oxford Review of Education*, 6(3): 255–78.

Palfreyman, D. (1989) The Warwick way: a case study of entrepreneurship within a university context, *Entrepreneurship and Regional Development*, 1(2): 207–19.

Palfreyman, D. and Warner, D. (eds) (1998) *Higher Education and the Law: A Guide for Managers.* Buckingham: SRHE/Open University Press.

Perrow, C. (1961) The analysis of goals in complex organizations, *American Sociological Review*, 26: 854–66.

Peters, T.J. and Waterman, R.H. (1982) *In Search of Excellence*. New York: HarperCollins.

Pfeffer, J. and Moore, W.L. (1980) Power in university budgeting: a replication and extension, *Administrative Science Quarterly*, 25: 637–53.

Pfeffer, J. and Salancik, G.R. (1974) Organisational decision making as a political process: the case of a university budget, *Administrative Science Quarterly*, 19: 135–51.

Psacharopoulos, G. (1990) Priorities in the financing of education, *International Journal of Educational Development*, 10(2/3).

Robbins, Lord (1963) *Report of the Committee on Higher Education under the Chairmanship of Lord Robbins*, Cmnd 2154. London: HMSO.

Robbins, S.P. (1990) *Organization Theory: Structure, Design, and Applications*. Englewood Cliffs, NJ: Prentice-Hall.

Salancik, G.R. and Pfeffer, J. (1974) The bases and use of power in organisational decision making: the case of a university, *Administrative Science Quarterly*, 19: 453–73.

Scapens, R.W., Ormston, A.L. and Arnold, J. (1994) The development of overhead recovery models at the University of Manchester, in R.H. Berry (ed.) *Management Accounting in Universities*. London: CIMA.

Schmidtlein, F.A. (1999) Assumptions underlying performance-based budgeting, *Tertiary Education and Management*, 5(2): 159–74.

Scott Morton, M.S. (1992) The effects of information technology on management and organizations, in T.A. Kochan and M. Useem (eds) *Transforming Organizations*. New York: Oxford University Press.

Sharpe, F. (1994) Devolution – towards a research framework, *Educational Management and Administration*, 22(2): 85–95.

Shattock, M.L. (1986) Implementing the Jarratt Report. Paper presented to a national conference on Jarratt organized by CIPFA, May 1986, quoted in D. Palfreyman (1989) The Warwick way: a case study of entrepreneurship within a university context, *Entrepreneurship and Regional Development*, 1(2): 207–19.

Shattock, M.L. (1988) Financial management in universities: the lessons from University College, Cardiff, *Financial Accountability and Management*, 4(2): 99–112.

Shattock, M.L. (1992) Higher education cuts, research selectivity and the management challenge, in E. Frackmann and P. Maassen *Towards Excellence in European Higher Education in the 90's*, chapter 13. Utrecht: Lemma and EAIR.

Shattock, M.L. (2000) Strategic management in European universities, *Tertiary Education and Management*, 6: 93–104.

Shattock, M.L. and Berdahl, R. (1985) The British University Grants Committee 1919–83: changing relationships with government and the universities, in I. McNay and J. Ozga (eds) *Policy-making in Education: The Breakdown of Consensus*, chapter 10. Oxford: Pergamon.

Shattock, M.L. and Rigby, F.G. (eds) (1983) *Resource Allocation in British Universities*. Guildford: SRHE.

Shinn, C.H. (1986) *Paying the Piper*. Lewes: Falmer Press.

Simon, H.A. (1961) *Administrative Behaviour*, 2nd edn. New York: Macmillan.

Simon, H.A. (1964) On the concept of organisational goal, *Administrative Science Quarterly*, 9: 1–22.

SORP (2000) *Statement of Recommended Practice: Accounting for Further and Higher Education*. London: CVCP.

Stacey, R.D. (1993) *Strategic Management and Organisational Dynamics*. London, Pitman.

Tapper, T. and Palfreyman, D. (1998) Continuity and change in the collegial tradition, *Higher Education Quarterly*, 52(2): 142–61.

Tapper, T. and Palfreyman, D. (2000) *Oxford and the Decline of the Collegiate Tradition*. Ilford: Woburn Press.

Teather, D.C.B. (ed.) (1999) *Higher Education in a Post-binary Era*. London: Jessica Kingsley.

Temple, P. and Whitchurch, C. (1994) The new entrepreneurship in British higher education, *Planning for Higher Education*, 22: 13–18.

Thomas, H.G. (1995) Implementing change: a case study of devolved formula-based resource allocation systems in two UK universities. Unpublished PhD thesis, Anglia Polytechnic University.

Thomas, H.G. (1996) Resource allocation in higher education: a cultural perspective, *Research in Post-compulsory Education*, 1(1): 35–51.

Thomas, H.G. (1997) The unexpected consequences of financial devolution, *Higher Education Review*, 29(3): 7–21.

Thomas, H.G. (1998) Reform and change in financial management: the need for an holistic approach, *Higher Education Management*, 10(2): 95–106.

Thomas, H.G. (1999) Managerial implications of adopting formula-based systems of resource allocation: a case study from higher education, *Educational Management and Administration*, 27(2): 183–91.

Thomas, H.G. (2000) Power in the resource allocation process: the impact of 'rational' systems, *Journal of Higher Education Policy and Management*, 22(2): 127–37.

Thompson, V.A. (1965) Bureaucracy and innovation, *Administrative Science Quarterly*, 10: 1–20.

Tomkins, C. and Mawditt, R. (1994) An attempt to introduce profit centre management within the University of Bath: a case study, in R.H. Berry (ed.) *Management Accounting in Universities*. London: CIMA.

Tomusk, V. (1995) 'Nobody can better destroy your higher education than yourself': critical remarks about quality assessment and funding in Estonian higher education, *Assessment and Evaluation in Higher Education*, 20(1): 115–24.

Tomusk, V. (1997), External quality assurance in Estonian higher education: its glory, take-off and crash, *Quality in Higher Education*, 3(2): 173–81.

Turner, C.M. (1992) *Power, Authority, Autonomy and Delegation: A Discursive Journey Round Some Big Words*. Bristol: The Staff College.

UFC (1989) *Research Selectivity Exercise, 1989: The Outcome (27/89)*. London: UFC.

UGC (1984) *A Strategy for Higher Education into the 1990s*. London: HMSO.

UGC (1986) *Planning for the Late 1980s: Recurrent Grant for 1986/87 (4/86)*. London: UGC.

University of Texas (1996) *Houston Statement on Governance*. http://oac.hsc.uth.tmc.edu/ut (accessed 7 September 1998).

Warner, D. and Palfreyman, D. (eds) (1996) *Higher Education Management: The Key Elements*. Buckingham: SRHE/Open University Press.

Warner, D. and Palfreyman, D. (eds) (2001) *The State of UK Higher Education*. Buckingham: SRHE/Open University Press.

Warwick, D. (1985) *The Times Higher Education Supplement*, 12 April, p. 8.

Watson, D. (2000) *Managing Strategy*. Buckingham: Open University Press.

Webber, G. (1998) Devolved budgeting – challenging the new orthodoxy, *perspectives: Policy and Practice in Higher Education*, 2(2): 64–7.

Weber, M. (1947) *The Theory of Social and Economic Organisation*, translated by A.R. Henderson and Talcott Parsons. London: William Hodge.

Weick, K.E. (1976) Educational organisations as loosely coupled systems, *Administrative Science Quarterly*, 21: 1–19.

Weiler, H.N. (2000) States, markets and university funding: new paradigms for the reform of higher education in Europe, *Compare*, 30(3): 333–9.

Welsh Office (1996) *Financial Memorandum between the Welsh Office and the Higher Education Funding Council for Wales*. Cardiff: Welsh Office.

Wildavsky, A. (1961) Political implications of budgetary reform, *Public Administration Review*, 21: 183–90.

Williams, G. (1990) The financial revolution at British universities, *Planning for Higher Education*, 19: 27–30.

Williams, G. (1992) *Changing Patterns of Finance in Higher Education*. Buckingham: SRHE/Open University Press.

Ziderman, A. and Albrecht, D. (1995) *Financing Universities in Developing Countries*. London: Falmer Press.

INDEX

Note: page numbers in *italics* refer to figures.

MANAGING THE ACADEMIC UNIT

Allan Bolton

As universities and colleges undergo significant change, then so do academic units (whether faculties, schools or departments) and the roles of their managers. *Managing the Academic Unit* explores these changes and tackles key issues such as devolution of responsibility, methods of decision making and formation of strategy. It is full of case study material which provides insider experience of, and practical advice for, running an academic unit. Allan Bolton gives guidance on key departmental concerns such as resource allocation, personnel, marketing, student recruitment, facilities and quality. He covers the varying needs of different academic units, from relatively well-developed and large schools to small departments and start-up operations. He also examines the qualities required of key players such as directors, deans, heads of department and faculty administrators, and presents ideas for improved induction and development opportunities for academic leaders.

Managing the Academic Unit is a key resource for actual and aspiring academic leaders. It provides both an overview and 'hands on' help for unit managers, and invites the 'head offices' of universities and colleges to reconsider ways to release the energy available in its academic units.

Contents
A world of change – Decision making – Allocating resources – Setting strategy – Staff roles – Business issues – Building a support team – Representing the unit – Benchmarking – Preparing to lead, manage and depart – Bibliography – Index.

176p   0 335 20404 X (Hardback)   0 335 20403 1 (Paperback)

MANAGING STRATEGY

David Watson

Higher education institutions are under increasing pressure to produce corporate and strategic plans, both for external audiences and for the internal purposes of setting and achieving goals. They are significantly dependent upon public investment and the expectations of public bodies, as well as upon a fast-changing market. David Watson sets out what strategic management can and should consist of in a modern, essentially democratic, university or college, and how to make it work. He examines:

- how universities and colleges should tailor corporate plans to satisfy external and internal requirements for their corporate plans
- how they should maximize their strategic assets and opportunities and minimize their weaknesses and threats;
- the role of governance and management in setting and achieving a strategic plan.

This book demonstrates how the academy must adapt to the needs of its rapidly changing host society as well as of a more diverse and plural internal community, whilst maintaining historical commitments. The result is an account of strategic management that is simultaneously careful of traditional values, restorative of those that have fallen into abeyance, and genuinely innovative.

Contents
Introduction – External perspectives – Internal perspectives – Personal perspectives – Appendix – References – Index.

176pp   0 335 20345 0 (Paperback)   0 335 20346 9 (Hardback)